A Native Plants Reader

Niall Dunne
Editor

BROOKLYN
BOTANIC
GARDEN

Elizabeth Peters
DIRECTOR OF DIGITAL
AND PRINT MEDIA

Dr. Susan Pell
SCIENCE EDITOR

Joni Blackburn
COPY EDITOR

Elizabeth Ennis
ART DIRECTOR

Scot Medbury
PRESIDENT

Elizabeth Scholtz
DIRECTOR EMERITUS

Handbook #197

Copyright © 2012 by Brooklyn Botanic Garden, Inc.

ISBN 978-1-889538-80-8

Printed in China by Ocean Graphics Press.

♲ Printed with soy-based inks on
postconsumer recycled paper.

Guides for a Greener Planet are published by
Brooklyn Botanic Garden, 1000 Washington Avenue,
Brooklyn, NY 11225.

Learn more at bbg.org/handbooks.

Cover: Isolated populations of native bloodroot (*Sanguinaria canadensis*) face many challenges to survival, but strategies like seed banking may help. Above: Habitat loss is the biggest threat to beautiful native wildflowers like redroot (*Lachnanthes caroliana*) and showy meadowbeauty (*Rhexia mariana*).

A Native Plants Reader

Introduction

Niall Dunne

In its celebrated series of handbooks, stretching back more than 60 years, Brooklyn Botanic Garden has long championed the use of native plants in the home garden. Guidebooks such as *Going Native* (1994), *Wildflower Gardens* (1999), and *Great Natives for Tough Places* (2009) have introduced gardeners to many spectacular and unusual North American species and taught them how to design beautiful, biodiverse, low-maintenance native plantings that impart a sense of place to their gardens and provide valuable resources for native birds, insects, and other wildlife.

A Native Plants Reader is a departure from the typical BBG handbook. Rather than offering a toolkit of growing tips and practical instructions, this book presents a collection of narratives extolling the virtues of natives, outlining their fundamental contributions to our natural ecosystems, detailing our connections with them, describing the perils they currently face, and advocating for their preservation in the garden and larger landscape. Chock-full of adventures and insights from scientists, gardeners, and writers working in the trenches with native plants, the essays are designed to address and engage both gardeners and nongardening nature lovers alike.

The 16 essays are loosely grouped into four themed sections: "Defining and Collecting," "Native Plants in Nature," "Native Plants in Gardens," and "Native Plants in Public." But the scope of the essays reaches well beyond simple classification, and there is a rich interpenetration of themes throughout the book. Beloved authors share their unique stories about what drew them to embrace native plants, and botanists and ecologists write about their experiences working in the field. Brooklyn Botanic Garden staff members discuss the significant contributions that BBG has been making to the field of native plant monitoring, conservation, and education since its founding a century ago. And in what is perhaps the key essay in the book, we learn about the challenges that native plants now face in the age of climate change, as well as some of the solutions that are being proposed.

All of the narratives sound a note of hope: hope that we recognize the uniqueness and beauty of our native flora and the vital services it performs. Hope that we invest the time, energy, money, and—for want of a better word—love that's needed to stop destroying our natural heritage, and start protecting it for future generations.

The lovely spring ephemeral Pacific trillium (*Trillium ovatum*) is native to the western U.S.; its eastern relative *Trillium grandiflorium* has vanished from New York City (see page 27).

Defining "Native Plant"

Niall Dunne

As an Irishman who just happened to be born in San Diego, was raised and grew to young manhood in Galway, Cork, and eventually Dublin, and also considers himself a New Yorker (some of the best years of my life!), I know something about the fuzziness that can surround discussions of nativeness. As a science writer and editor specializing in plants and plant ecology, I'm also aware of the imprecision that plagues the term "native plant" and the flotilla of definitions for it bobbing out there in the Google-sphere—enough to drive an Irish Californian New Yorker like myself to drink!

The definitions of "native plant" put out by U.S. government agencies and scientific institutions are motivated not by nationalistic pride or sentimentality but by a pressing need to identify and monitor our native biodiversity in a scientifically verifiable way, and preserve it in the face of very real threats, such as habitat loss, invasive species, and climate change. Most of these definitions are strongly similar. To give some examples, according to Executive Order 13112, signed in 1999 by President Clinton, " 'Native species' means, with respect to a particular ecosystem, a species that, other than as a result of introduction, historically occurred or currently occurs in that ecosystem." The National Park Service defines natives as "all species that have occurred or now occur as a result of natural processes on lands designated as units of the national park system." The USDA's PLANTS website says a plant is native to the U.S. if it was "naturally occurring at the time of Columbus."

The definition we use in this handbook is that put forward by the Plant Conservation Alliance, a consortium of 10 federal agencies and more than 200 nonfederal collaborators (including Brooklyn Botanic Garden): *A native (indigenous) species is one that occurs in a particular region, ecosystem, and habitat without direct or indirect human actions. Species native to North America are generally recognized as those occurring on the continent prior to European settlement.*

Natural Occurrence

All these definitions share the basic concept that native species are those that occur in an area or ecosystem without having been introduced by humans. Admittedly, this is a pretty broad idea. And it's not invulnerable to criticism: Ever since *Homo*

The United States Fish and Wildlife Service lists hart's tongue fern (*Asplenium scolopendrium* var. *americanum*) as native in New York State. This rare plant is also federally protected.

sapiens arrived on the scene at least 150,000 years ago, we've been moving plants around the planet (intentionally or not)—and it's difficult to trace the exact origins of some of these species.

Some definitions contain an evolutionary component in an attempt to circumvent this confusion. Saying that a native plant is one that "evolved naturally" in a particular region adds a flavor of deep geologic time to the definition. But this supposed clarification is not without its problems. Fossil records of plants or pollen can be incomplete or difficult to interpret. Moreover, environmental adaptation in plants and other organisms doesn't necessarily take a long time to occur. Indeed, rapid evolution is quite common among nonnative invasive species due to increased selection pressure in the novel environments they colonize.

To simplify matters somewhat, most U.S. definitions for "native plant" only take into account the human-caused introductions that have taken place in and after 1492, the year Christopher Columbus first reached the North American continent. This is not an arbitrary date, or one meant to trivialize the assisted migration of plants that occurred prior to European settlement. Though precolonial Native Americans undoubtedly moved plants into and around the continent (for example, corn—domesticated in present-day Mexico—had become a dietary staple in eastern North America by the time the first Europeans arrived, and papaya had most likely been brought to Florida from the Caribbean), these introductions were on a much smaller scale compared with those that have taken place within the past 500 years.

The so-called Columbian Exchange, an era of rapid exchange of plants and animals between the Old and New Worlds, wrought dramatic cultural and biological change all around the globe. Botanists acknowledge the importance of this exchange even in Europe, where plants have been introduced and moved around for many millennia, distinguishing between ancient nonnative plants, or archaeophytes, and nonnatives introduced from 1492 onward, neophytes.

Importance of Geographical Scale

When we talk about nonnative plants, generally we're referring to species that have been introduced to the country from distant lands. But technical definitions of nativeness operate on multiple geographical scales, so it's possible for a plant to be native to one U.S. state but not another. For instance, northern spicebush (*Lindera benzoin*) is an enchanting shrub indigenous to a large portion of the eastern U.S. In general terms, it qualifies as a U.S. native; however, when you apply our chosen definition above, the species is clearly only native to one half of the country and is nonnative to other (that is, the western U.S.). If you search for *Lindera benzoin* on the USDA's PLANTS Database (plants.usda.gov) and examine the maps (the species maps chart both native status and distribution), you'll see that the plant is also nonnative to some eastern states as well, including Wisconsin and Minnesota.

"Invasive Plants" and "Weeds"

Sarah Reichard

The term "invasive plant" can cause confusion because people tend to use it differently in different circumstances. "Invasive" is sometimes used to describe native plants that naturally colonize plant communities in which they were not previously growing, such as trees "invading" grasslands; however, this is just an example of natural succession from one community type to another, and these trees should not be labeled as "invasive species." Native plants such as poison ivy (*Toxicodendron radicans*) and boxelder (*Acer negundo*) that tend to grow en masse in disturbed areas are sometimes erroneously called invasive, when in fact these plants are early successional species whose populations thin and in some cases disappear in mature forest habitats.

In recent years, the term "invasive" has become synonymous with nonnative, "alien," or "exotic" species that enter native ecosystems (usually with help from humans) and degrade them by competing with native species for resources such as nutrients, water, sunlight, and space. Gardeners sometime conflate the terms "invasive" and "weed"; however, "weed" cannot be defined biologically. There are as many definitions of weed as there are weeds, but a good one is a plant that is growing where you don't want it to grow! "Noxious weeds" are those that have legal standing, meaning they've been designated as harmful by county, state, or federal authorities and are regulated. They usually include plant species that are considered injurious to humans or to our economic interests, such as agriculture, aquatic ecosystems, and the preservation of wildlands.

Keeping native successional species, invasive species, and weeds straight can be a real headache, but doing so will help you make more informed landscape management decisions.

If gardeners in Minnesota are growing northern spicebush in their yards, by definition they're growing a nonnative plant, even though the species is native in neighboring Iowa and Illinois. Of course, using political boundaries to delineate nativity is artificial. Plants and animals don't recognize county, state, or national borders—their patterns of distribution are determined by geophysical and biological factors.

Our definition of a native species logically determines our definition of a nonnative species, and it's integral to our definition of what constitutes an invasive species. The vast majority of invasive plants in this country come from other continents; however, some native plants have distributions that stretch far beyond our continental borders. It's also possible for a plant native in one area of the U.S. to be nonnative in another, or, on a smaller geographical scale, to be native in one part of a state and nonnative in another. For example, the yellow bush lupine (*Lupinus arboreus*), which is native to coastal scrub and sand dunes in southern and central California, is invasive in dune ecosystems of northern California, Oregon, and Washington, where it was widely introduced for its attractive yellow flowers and dune-stabilizing abilities but is now outcompeting indigenous dune vegetation.

Defining species as native only within their current regional ranges, even when we allow for natural fluctuations at the extreme edges of these ranges, is another broad simplification, because it ignores the slow migrations that many of these species have undergone as a result of naturally occurring changes in climate over time. During the Pleistocene epoch, which ended around 12,000 years ago, repeated glaciations caused frequent range shifts in native plants and animals. Some definitions of a native plant—a couple of which I included earlier—incorporate the idea of historical occurrence. But they beg the question of how far back in time we should go. For example, 10,000 years ago, the ice sheets of the Wisconsin glaciation stretched as far south as present-day New Jersey: Should we then consider the Arctic plants that migrated southward in advance of the glaciers and then northward again as they retreated native to New Jersey? And what about extant species that grew here in ancient times but eventually died out? Few would argue that dawn redwood (*Metasequoia glyptostroboides*), which flourished across North America tens of millions of years ago but is today found growing naturally only in China, still counts as a U.S. native.

Local Genotypes

Another important shortcoming in most native plant definitions is that they don't account for the existence of genetic variation within individual plant species. Most species are genetically variable, and distinct populations of a plant often have genetic differences that make them better adapted to their local environmental conditions. Restoration ecologists typically use locally sourced plants when replanting a forest or other habitat because it increases their chances of a successful restoration and also preserves the genetic integrity of nearby populations of the same species. Using plants or seeds from nonlocal sources carries the risk of "outbreeding depression"—whereby the blending of locally adapted and nonlocal genotypes results in a population of plants that's less fit for survival.

The idea of a native genotype is a further refinement of the concept of a native species. Some people would argue that "native" only really makes sense if it's "locally native." Others would say this only matters for restoration professionals and gardeners who live in close proximity to wilderness areas. In her book *The Conscientious Gardener*, Sarah Reichard argues that gardeners living near wild plants should use caution when it comes to the provenance of their native plants and seeds in order to avoid genetically polluting wild neighbors.

This caveat extends to cultivars of native plants. Though cultivated selections of wild plants are technically native, they are essentially clones of a single individual plant and contain little genetic variation. In addition, gardeners often use cultivars selected from areas outside their own region. For example, *Magnolia grandiflora* 'Little Gem', a widely grown dwarf cultivar of the southern magnolia, was selected from a North Carolina parent plant. As such, it may not be optimally adapted to growing in Florida, say, and may pose a threat to wild populations of southern magnolia there.

Even for gardeners who don't live close to wild native plants, it's still generally a good idea to grow native plants of local provenance because they are more likely to perform well in your regional climate (and if a bird does happen to transfer a seed from your yard into a natural area, there's no cause for alarm). Red maple is an interesting example. One of the most widespread native hardwood trees in North America, it can be found growing from Quebec and Ontario south to Florida and west to Texas in a wide variety of soil and site conditions. Researchers have identified several ecotypes—genetically and physiologically distinct populations adapted to different environmental extremes—of this plant across its range. Gardeners in cold northern climes may have little success with a red maple ecotype adapted to the sultry Southeast.

Climate Change: A Challenge to Current Definitions

In the coming years, as more and more native plants respond to climate change and shift their ranges, our current definitions will be put to the test. Plants are already on the move. For example, a 2010 study in the Siskiyou Mountains of Oregon found that over a 65-year period, because of the increasingly drier climate, the composition of understory herb communities in lower montane forest has changed to resemble that of more drought-tolerant communities from farther south.

If we strictly apply our current definitions, native plants that shift their ranges due to climate change will technically be "nonnative" in these newly adopted territories. This could create a classification and conservation nightmare, and it seems to be the general feeling among scientists that we'll have to modify our current definitions to take human-caused climate change into account.

"Few would argue that a species becomes a nonnative if it migrates to a new region because its climate envelope has shifted to the new region," says Louis Pitelka, professor emeritus at the University of Maryland's Center for Environmental Studies. "There will be many significant shifts in the distributions of major ecosystem types." The bigger issue, he says, is how well our native species will be able to disperse across our fragmented landscapes in order to survive—and how well they'll be able to compete against invasives that will also be on the move. Says Pitelka, "Climate change may favor highly invasive species and make it more difficult for slower migrating, less aggressive native species to establish in new areas."

Perhaps it is and will always be impossible to come up with a perfect definition of a native plant. Such is the challenge of boiling down complex phenomena into simple formulae. Nonetheless, as long as we understand the backstory and can justify our generalizations—and modify them when necessary—it can be useful to agree on valid, short-form working definitions such as the one we employ in this book.

Early Botanical Exploration and Discovery in the Northeast

James L. Reveal

For much of my career at the University of Maryland, I did research out West, studying the plants of the Intermountain Region. At least I did until a newly arrived dean decided that I should devote more time to the native flora of Maryland. Consequently, I spent much of the 1980s working in England. Why England? Because that's where some of the earliest collections of temperate North American plants are preserved—in the herbaria of the Linnaean Society and the Natural History Museum, the Royal Botanic Gardens, Kew (all in London), and Oxford University. The first wave of pioneer naturalists that explored the flora and fauna of the Northeast sent what they collected back home to Europe to be cataloged and—in many cases—named.

Seeds and specimens of many of the early plants found in the Northeast initially arrived in Europe from what is now Canada, with the majority going to gardens in France. The first explorers of the New World were mainly interested in plants for their medicinal potential, but the French were also intrigued with trees that could either improve their naval stores or had horticultural appeal.

The first major formal effort to account for plants of the Northeast was the 1635 illustrated *Canadensium Plantarum Historia*. Written by the French physician Jacques Philippe Cornut (1606–1651), it described 38 collected species growing in the gardens of the Faculty of Medicine, Paris, including red trillium (*Trillium erectum*) and starry false lily-of-the-valley (*Maianthemum stellatum*). A few decades later, the English traveler John Josselyn (1638–1675) published his *New England's Rarities Discovered* and described and illustrated numerous new species of plants, including skunk cabbage (*Symplocarpus foetidus*). Although his descriptions were poor and his drawings crude, Josselyn's work was the most complete summary of the North American flora until the Linnaean era of the mid-18th century.

The latter half of the 17th century was a period of great botanical exploration in the Northeast, particularly in the middle Atlantic region (stretching from what is now New York south to Virginia). Members of the Royal Society of London, founded in 1660, paid settlers, travelers, and adventurers to send specimens for their museums

One of America's early naturalists, William Bartram (1739–1823), along with his father, John, discovered more than 200 plant species previously unknown by European botanists.

and seeds for their private gardens. Foremost in providing specimens was the English clergyman John Banister (1650–1692), who roamed the forests of Virginia for plants and insects. He sent home nearly 400 plant species that were referenced in the preparation of some seminal works, including John Ray's three-volume global treatment of all known plants of his day, *Historia Generalis Plantarum* (1686–1704).

Hazards of Exploration

Examining Banister's exceptional drawings and dried specimens in London and at Oxford was a moving experience for me. To actually touch Banister's specimen of *Aquilegia canadensis* (red columbine) or see his drawing of *Dodecatheon meadia* (Eastern shooting-star) always brought chills. Banister was planning to write his own natural history of Virginia, but his life was cut short in 1692, when he was accidentally shot by a hunter during a field trip along the Roanoke River.

The dangers of exploration in eastern North America were real. Injuries, drowning, and disease posed the most serious threats. There was also the risk of attack by local natives, who sometimes sought revenge against the injustices brought upon them by white settlers. John Lawson (1674–1711), who arrived from England shortly after the death of Banister and led natural history expeditions through the wilderness of the Carolinas, suffered such a fate. While ascending the Neuse River in 1711, he was captured by the Tuscarora Indians, tortured, and burned at the stake.

The vagaries of sea travel also wreaked havoc on the work of some colonial explorers. In the early 1740s, the plant collector Cadwallader Colden (1688–1776), who eventually became governor of New York, sent a large collection of dried specimens supporting a series of novel plant descriptions to the Swedish botanist Carl Linnaeus (1707–1778)—but the ship was captured by pirates, and most of the collection never made it to Europe. The explorer Constantine Rafinesque (1783–1840) was shipwrecked not far out of New York in 1815 and lost everything—his fortune, his collection of plants and animals spanning 20 years, his books, and manuscripts. He also lost his wife, who was in Sicily at the time and—upon hearing of her husband's misfortune—ran off with an actor.

The Linnaean Era

In 1990 and 1991, I worked on the Natural History Museum's Linnaean Plant Name Typification Project, reviewing the specimens used by Linnaeus to describe plants from temperate North America. Linnaeus's influence on early botanical explorations in the Northeast cannot be overstated. Starting in 1735 with the publication of *Systema Naturae*, he embarked on his monumental effort to revolutionize the way biologists classify the natural world—and to describe as many of its life forms as possible. Naturalists sent him plant and animal specimens from the four corners of the globe.

Most of the plants available to Linnaeus from North America were gathered in the mid-Atlantic and southern colonies, so he sent one of his students, Pehr Kalm (1716–1779), to venture from Pennsylvania to southeastern Canada in search of new species. From 1748 to 1751, Kalm wandered through the forests of the Northeast, using the Swedish-Finnish settlement of Raccoon (now Swedesboro), New Jersey, as his base of operations. He is credited as the first trained scientist to write a description of the Niagara Falls. Kalm returned with several hundred plants for Linnaeus, who recognized him by naming one of the Northeast's most beautiful native shrubs in his honor: mountain laurel, *Kalmia latifolia*.

About the time that the Linnaean era began, there was a shift in the horticultural demands for plants in Europe. By then, estate grounds had been planted with an abundance of trees and shrubs, but the addition of formal roads and paths created a demand for border plants. Colorful annuals and herbaceous perennials that could be grown rapidly and easily transplanted at different seasons of the year became the fashion. Suddenly, there was renewed interest in the flora of eastern North America, with its wealth of flowering herbs.

The Bartrams of Philadelphia

Enter John Bartram (1699–1777)—America's first homegrown naturalist—of King-sessing, a small village along the Schuylkill River near Philadelphia. While others collected specimens in Virginia, Bartram did the same in the north, but with decidedly greater skill and devotion. Bartram's travels took him throughout most of the American colonies, where he gathered seeds and in some cases, live plants. By growing these seeds and plants on his farm, he was able to obtain an abundance of plant material to sell to wealthy gentlemen of England, earning enough money to support his summer forays about the colonies. He was eventually granted an annual stipend of 50 pounds by King George III, as well as the title "King's Botanist." With one of his sons, William (1739–1823), Bartram would dominate North American botany for half a century.

The Bartrams discovered more than 200 plant species that were later described and named by European botanists. These included the Venus flytrap (*Dionaea muscipula*), native to the Carolinas and formally named in 1768 by English merchant and botanist John Ellis after the Greek goddess of love, the daughter of Dione. At Oxford 200 years later, examining the Bartrams' collections transported me—seeing John's bold handwriting in goose-quilled ink, I pictured him toiling away by the lantern light of his home late on a winter's night.

Muhlenberg, Michaux, Pursh, and Nuttall

A new era in American floristics began after the Revolutionary War, as taxonomy moved from a science dominated by Europeans to one championed by Americans. The era also saw the development of our own universities, libraries, scientific societies (most notably the American Philosophical Society, founded in 1743 by Benjamin Franklin), and even herbaria. One of the more influential early American botanists was Gotthilf Muhlenberg (1753–1815), who worked as a Lutheran pastor in the town of Lancaster, Pennsylvania. Muhlenberg discovered more than 100 new species (most of which were formally described later by others) close to his home and kept a meticulously maintained herbarium. He was an inspiration for all other American botanists that followed.

European naturalists continued to travel to North America to make a name for themselves or find useful plants to take back home. One of the most famous was the French botanist André Michaux (1746–1802), who arrived in 1785 as an emissary of King Louis XVI, charged with finding plants that could be used for carpentry, medicine, and pasture forage in France. His travels over the next several years took him from Canada to Florida and west into Kentucky and Illinois. He named many new species during his time in America and sent home 90 cases of seeds and plants to France. In 1803, Michaux published his *Flora Boreali-Americana*, the first full treatment of the known plants of eastern North America.

Almost immediately, criticisms were leveled at the book, the most serious of them being Michaux's failure to examine collections in England and thus to account for several new species known there but not yet in France. The American botanist Benjamin Smith Barton (1766–1815) of the University of Pennsylvania also noted a number species that Michaux had failed to include. A friend of Thomas Jefferson and William Bartram, Barton urged his students and others to collect in the western part of the new United States, which after the Louisiana Purchase of 1803 stretched all the way to modern-day Montana and Wyoming. Barton authored the first American botanical textbook, *Elements of Botany* (1803), but he is probably best remembered for supporting the activities of two much more accomplished European botanists, Frederick Pursh (1774–1820) and Thomas Nuttall (1786–1859).

Trained as a gardener, the Saxony-born Pursh came to the United States around 1799 and took employment at various estates in Baltimore and Philadelphia until he was hired in 1805 by Barton as a part-time curator and collector. Over the next five years Pursh collected around the Northeast—finding such diverse new plants as the northern water plantain (*Alisma triviale*) and common juniper (*Juniperus communis* var. *depressa*)—worked various odd jobs (a personal battle with alcoholism prevented him from holding down steady work), and assembled specimens from all over North America, including a number from the Lewis and Clark Expedition. In 1811, he traveled to London, where he caused a scandal among his gentleman colleagues by marrying a barmaid. In December 1813, he published his *Flora Americae Septentrionalis*, the first attempt at a continent-wide flora.

His achievement was marred by controversy, however. Pursh was accused by fellow botanists, particularly Thomas Nuttall, of acquiring plant specimens that others had collected, describing them without their approval, and taking all the credit for himself. Not long after his flora was published, Pursh was informally exiled from the botanical community. He subsequently traveled to Canada in 1816 with the hopes of reviving his career by writing a flora specifically for Canada, only to have his library and newly gathered herbarium burn in a fire two years later. Pursh died, destitute and alone, in Montreal in 1820.

If that weren't punishment enough for poor old Pursh, his flora was quickly superseded by that of his rival, Thomas Nuttall. A Yorkshire native, Nuttall arrived in Philadelphia in 1808 and was hired almost immediately by Barton, who sent him to collect in Delaware and along the Chesapeake Bay, and soon after that, around the Great Lakes region. In 1811, Nuttall took an unscheduled detour up the Missouri River with a fur trapping company and discovered numerous new species, many of potential horticultural importance, including large beardtongue (*Penstemon grandiflorus*) and soapweed yucca (*Yucca glauca*). In 1818, Nuttall published *The Genera of North American Plants* in two volumes, replacing the works of both Michaux and Pursh as the authoritative flora of the Northeast.

Paving the Way for the Next Generation

One more botanist from this era deserves a special mention: Amos Eaton (1776–1842) of New York. A lawyer by profession, he was jailed in 1810 on charges of forgery in a land dispute. He spent nearly five years in prison, during which time he taught himself botany and geology and prepared a regional flora based on Linnaeus's system of classification. He also tutored and taught botany to the prison inspector's son, a certain John Torrey (1796–1873), who went on to become one of the most distinguished botanists of the 19th century and to found the first botanical society in the Americas, now known as the Torrey Botanical Society. After his release from prison, Eaton published his *Manual of Botany for the Northern States* (1817), which informed the next generation of American botanists, including Asa Gray (1810–1888), Darwin's great champion in the United States; Torrey (who, along with Gray, published the definitive *Flora of North America* in the late 1830s and early 1840s); and Nathaniel Lord Britton (1859–1934), first director of the New York Botanical Garden, which now houses the largest herbarium in the Western Hemisphere.

Walking through the forests around my hometown of Ithaca, New York, I see numerous trees and shrubs that were named by Linnaeus, Michaux, Pursh, or Nuttall. In some cases I know the plant's history: who found it, when it arrived in Europe, and how it was that Linnaeus in particular came to have knowledge of the species. Looking about my own 11-acre garden, I also see native plants named by each of these botanical pioneers, as well as several collected by Pehr Kalm, who passed nearby on one of his trips to Canada. All the plants found by the early collectors and named by the first taxonomists are special to me—each has a history just waiting to be told.

The Metropolitan Flora
Susan K. Pell and Steven Glenn

Many people are surprised to learn that there are botanists employed in New York City. They think of Gotham as consisting only of millions of people and thousands of acres of pavement—and perhaps a few dogs to relieve themselves on that pavement! However, more than 500 community gardens thrive in NYC, and the city's Department of Parks and Recreation and the National Park Service together oversee more than 50,000 acres of land, much of which is green space. Parks and gardens are just the publicly managed land—thousands of additional wild acres are scattered throughout the five boroughs. Altogether these lands support approximately 1,000 native plant species, which are the subject of some serious botanical study.

When the entire metropolitan area is considered, the flora is even more diverse and includes roughly 3,000 native and naturalized (nonnative but growing on their own outside cultivation) plant species. The New York Metropolitan Flora Project (NYMF) at Brooklyn Botanic Garden (BBG) is a multiyear effort to document these native and introduced plants. Scientists at BBG have been surveying the flora that grows naturally within a 50-mile radius of the city (an area of approximately 7,650 square miles) since the project began in 1990 under the direction of Dr. Steven Clemants. It is the longest-running research project at BBG and the largest effort of its kind in North America. Most regional floras specify species occurrence down to the county level, but the NYMF project looks at plant distributions on a much finer scale—its range is divided into 967 five- by five-kilometer ($25 km^2$) plots.

Intensive field surveys in spring, summer, and fall are combined with data-gathering trips to regional herbaria (natural history collections of preserved plant specimens) in winter to draw a complete picture of both the present-day and historic floras of the NYMF range. The earliest herbarium specimens included in the NYMF data are two 1804 beaked spikerush (*Eleocharis rostellata*) collections—one from Richmond, Staten Island, and the other from Flushing, Queens—and the most recent specimens are being collected now, five days a week during the field season (roughly March to November). The initial products of the project are available on Brooklyn Botanic Garden's website (bbg.org/research/nymf) and include current and historic distribution maps of each species as well as county-level species-occurrence lists.

Steven Glenn, manager of the New York Metropolitan Flora Project, collects a native euphorbia for BBG's herbarium.

Many insights can be gained from analyzing the range maps. For instance, we can detect the different habitat preferences of closely related plant species, the flora's response to climate change, and the extent of the invasion of introduced plant species. We can also determine which native plants have become exceedingly rare in the area since 1979, the last year included in the historic distribution maps.

Mapping Nonnative Invasions

Invasive species are among the greatest threats to our native ecosystems. They crowd out native plants, often do not provide suitable food and shelter for native insects and other animals, and can alter the foundational structure of an ecosystem. In addition, they usually come to foreign lands without their natural pests and competing species, both of which keep plant populations in check in their native ranges.

A prime example of an invasive species that exhibits all of these unfortunate qualities is garlic mustard (*Alliaria petiolata*), an introduced plant from Eurasia that colonizes and degrades ecosystems across North America. This herbaceous plant not only produces an enormous number of seeds that germinate in the early spring when competition is low in the forest understory and in open areas such as roadsides, it also releases compounds from its roots that alter the microbial diversity of the soil, making the plant a more effective invader. These compounds also have allelopathic properties—that is, they inhibit the growth of plants in the soils in which they are released. Thus, wherever garlic mustard invades, it changes the community structure of the habitat, from the microscopic level up.

The distribution map for *Alliaria petiolata* shows that before 1980 this plant was found in only a handful of places in the metropolitan area, but since that time it has spread throughout the NYMF range and is now one of the most common flowering herbaceous species in the flora. Reassessments of plots not recently visited are expected to show even wider distribution of this pest.

Similar trends are seen with other notorious invaders in the region. The well-known multiflora rose (*Rosa multiflora*), tree-of-heaven (*Ailanthus altissima*), Norway maple (*Acer platanoides*), Oriental bittersweet (*Celastrus orbiculata*), Japanese barberry (*Berberis thunbergii*), Japanese honeysuckle (*Lonicera japonica*), and Morrow's honey-suckle (*L. morrowii*) all occur in nearly every surveyed plot across the region.

The NYMF team has also mapped more recently introduced nonnative species for which very few historic (pre-1980) records exist within the flora area. These include broadleaf helleborine (*Epipactis helleborine*), an invasive orchid often mistaken as native; small carpetgrass (*Arthraxon hispidus*), an Asian grass first reported in the U.S. in 1877, in Pennsylvania, but which has only recently become problematic in the NYMF range; and Japanese angelica tree (*Aralia elata*), which had been misidentified as devil's walking stick (*A. spinosa*), a southeastern relative, until NYMF scientists collected the plant in flower and made the correct species determination.

Mapping Species Distribution Changes

Findings of BBG's New York Metropolitan Flora Project serve as vital references for people concerned with native species conservation, habitat restoration, and the long-term health of ecosystems. Below are four examples of the stories that NYMF data have provided about changing plant populations.

American Bittersweet (*Celastrus scandens*)

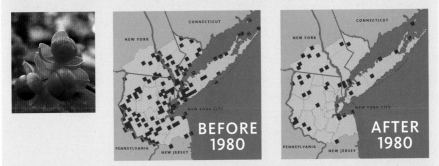

American bittersweet is an attractive and innocuous vine that is becoming so rare in New York State that it is designated as "Exploitably Vulnerable." NYMF data show how the local species distribution has declined over time.

Oriental Bittersweet (*Celastrus orbiculatus*)

Oriental bittersweet is among America's most noxious invasives. The rampant vine wraps so tightly around host trees that it can girdle and strangle them. Although superficially similar to American bittersweet, a number of features give this exotic an edge over its native relative: brighter berries that attract more bird dispersers; a greater number of seeds; and more efficient photosynthesis, which allows it to grow more rapidly with a shorter winter dormancy. This pest plant is now found in almost every part of the NYMF study area.

Tuberous Grasspink (*Calopogon tuberosus*)

This beautiful orchid once grew profusely in the wetlands where JFK International Airport now sits; today it is one of about 100 native species showing marked decline in the area of the NYMF study. The cause? Most likely habitat loss, specifically the loss to urban development of Atlantic white cedar swamps and wetlands.

Marsh-Speedwell (*Veronica scutellata*)

Marsh-speedwell (*Veronica scutellata*), native to most of Canada and the northern United States, is another herbaceous perennial that prefers wetland habitats. NYMF data show that populations have shifted north over the past 30 years, a migration that could be related to climate change. Mountain maple (*Acer spicatum*), New Jersey tea (*Ceanothus americanus*), and bunchberry dogwood (*Cornus canadensis*) are other native species that display a northward shift in distribution in the NYMF study.

Unfortunately, exotic invasive species that typically grew south of the region, such as camphorweed (*Heterotheca subaxillaris*) and kudzu (*Pueraria montana*), seem to be migrating north as well. As the climate changes, New York's native flora may face increasing competition from these and other aggressive species that up until recently had been kept in check by colder New York winters.

At the cutting edge of invasive species studies, the NYMF data are revealing newly introduced nonnative species that have become widespread in the metropolitan area and may become more problematic in the near future. These species are not known to have occurred in the area before 1980. Many of them are already well established in the range, such as narrowleaf bittercress (*Cardamine impatiens*), Nepalese browntop (*Microstegium vimineum*), and Japanese holly (*Ilex crenata*). Others are just making their way into the range but are plants to watch out for because their distributions are likely to expand. Some examples include waterthyme (*Hydrilla verticillata*), a federally listed noxious weed so far known from only four records in the area but hugely troublesome everywhere else it has been introduced; water chestnut (*Trapa natans*), now distributed widely, but not commonly, within the range thanks to its water-dispersed fruits; Asiatic tearthumb, also called mile-a-minute weed (*Polygonum perfoliatum*), notable for its triangular leaves and abundant prickles; and hairy crabweed (*Fatoua villosa*), an invasive in the Southeast and Midwest but currently only known in the Northeast from two records on Long Island. Any of these plants could be the next major invasive threat to the native landscape in the Northeast.

Decline of the Native

Coupled with the ever-growing presence of invasive species in the New York metropolitan area is the decline of many of our native plant species. To date, the NYMF project has identified nearly 100 species that show serious reductions in distribution. For example, as the range and abundance of invasive Oriental bittersweet and Morrow's honeysuckle has increased, there has been a documented and undoubtedly correlated population decrease in their closely related natives American bittersweet (*Celastrus scandens*) and limber honeysuckle (*Lonicera dioica*).

Of course, the threats to native species are varied: In addition to competition from invasive plants, they have to deal with such insults as climate change, exotic animal pests, the deer population explosion, and land development. Then there are all the challenges of city life: compacted soils; high levels of salt from snow-melting efforts; increased average temperatures from the heat island effect; air, water, and soil pollution; and assault from the tetrapod residents. All these threats are directly or indirectly due to human activities.

Ironically, among the species declining under these human-made pressures and slipping out of the NYMF range are some of our most beloved wildflowers: tuberous grasspink orchid (*Calopogon tuberosus*), bunchberry dogwood (*Cornus canadensis*), swamp-pink (*Helonias bullata*), wood lily (*Lilium philadelphicum*), brown widelip orchid (*Liparis liliifolia*), phlox species (*Phlox subulata* and *P. pilosa*), gentians (*Gentiana andrewsii* and *G. saponaria*), azaleas (*Rhododendron canadense* and *R. prinophyllum*), and trilliums (*Trillium cernuum* and *T. undulatum*).

Detecting Responses to Climate Change

Some plant populations are able to respond to human-caused threats through their innate tolerance of environmental changes—by evolving tolerance for new conditions or resistance to new pests, or simply by establishing populations at higher elevation or latitude as the climate in their current ranges heats up. Unfortunately, others are devastated by these new challenges—often to the point of extirpation.

Climate change appears to be one of the threats to which at least some of our native plants can respond rather quickly. The NYMF data show a number of native species whose distributions have shifted north over the past 30 years, either heading out of or moving in to the New York metropolitan area. These include mountain maple (*Acer spicatum*), bog rosemary (*Andromeda glaucophylla*), water arum (*Calla palustris*), New Jersey tea (*Ceanothus americanus*), marsh-speedwell (*Veronica scutellata*), longbract frog orchid (*Coeloglossum viride*), bunchberry dogwood (*Cornus canadensis*), plains snakecotton (*Froelichia floridana*), creeping snowberry (*Gaultheria hispidula*), bog laurel (*Kalmia polifolia*), water loosestrife (*Lysimachia thyrsiflora*), buckbean (*Menyanthes trifoliata*), and early azalea (*Rhododendron prinophyllum*).

Unfortunately, we are seeing similar migrations of exotic invasive species as well—camphorweed golden-aster (*Heterotheca subaxillaris*) and kudzu (*Pueraria montana*) are two examples—demonstrating that escaping one threat does not necessarily protect you from another!

Niches and Habitat Preferences

Beyond looking at the geographic distribution patterns of plants in the NYMF data to see where species are found or how they have redistributed within the range, we can also look for geographic and biological factors that are correlated with these distributions. For example, some species clearly have particular soil or other habitat preferences. Within the NYMF range, maidenhair spleenwort (*Asplenium trichomanes*) and chinkapin oak (*Quercus muehlenbergii*) are most abundant on the calcareous (chalky) soils of the Franklin Marble region in northern Warren and southern Sussex counties in New Jersey. Several species clearly prefer growing in sandy coastal soils: American beachgrass (*Ammophila breviligulata*), bearberry (*Arctostaphylos uva-ursi*), and post oak (*Quercus stellata*) are some examples.

Saltmarsh-elder (*Iva frutescens*) grows only in brackish water, and American water-willow (*Justicia americana*) is restricted to a few sections along the Delaware River. The latter's very limited freshwater distribution within the NYMF range is perhaps due to the specific water chemistry of the Delaware. Interestingly, American water-willow was historically also found along the Delaware and Raritan Canal, built in the 1830s to connect the Delaware and Raritan rivers, but these populations cannot be located today and are likely gone. It may be that the initial water chemistry of the canal was similar to that of the Delaware but changed over time and no longer provides a suitable habitat for this aquatic plant species.

Comparing the different habitat preferences of closely related native species can provide insight into how organisms carve out niches for themselves and thus how populations evolve into new species. There are several examples of such species in the NYMF data, including the widespread maleberry (*Lyonia ligustrina*) and the related coast-loving staggerbush (*L. mariana*), which is restricted to sandy coastal soils. Similarly, common elderberry (*Sambucus canadensis*) is extremely widespread, whereas red elderberry (*S. racemosa*) prefers the highlands. Two *Corylus* species, American filbert (*C. americana*) and beaked hazel (*C. cornuta*), as well as two *Prunus* species, chokecherry (*P. virginiana*) and black cherry (*P. serotina*), show similar generalist versus highland patterns; American filbert and black cherry are much more common and widespread than closely related species. In fact, black cherry is the most common woody species in the NYMF range (the notorious poison ivy, *Toxicodendron radicans*, is the second most common).

The Future of NYMF

Brooklyn Botanic Garden scientists have learned a great deal about the New York metropolitan flora by creating detailed species-distribution maps; however, we are poised to understand even more about the intricacies of this flora and its ability to respond to human-induced and natural pressures. Data and analytical techniques now exist that were nearly inconceivable when the NYMF project began, more than 20 years ago. Analyzing the NYMF data in the context of modern geographic information system (GIS) tools and technology will expose the factors involved in species distributions and ecosystem dynamics. It will allow us to understand the numerous connections between plant distributions and, for example, geography, soil type, temperature, precipitation, land development, and deer and human population densities.

The results of these analyses will be used to project species migrations, predict potential distributions of newly arrived invasive species, identify locations to search for populations of rare plants and suitable locations for the reintroduction of regionally extirpated plants, and generally inform conservation and development efforts. The future of the New York Metropolitan Flora Project lies in mining the data for the story of how and why native and exotic plant species have moved around this area in response to interactions with the land and its many inhabitants. The legacy of the project will be what we, and future generations, do with this knowledge.

New York City's Vanished Natives

Mariellé Anzelone
Illustrations by Wendy Hollender

When you stand in the middle of Times Square, it's easy to forget that the European colonists (and before them, the Lenape) settled in Manhattan because of its bounty of natural resources. Before there were skyscrapers and restaurants, New York City's wealth was measured in flora and fauna. Early Dutch sailors were disoriented by the scent of wildflowers wafting out to sea from the island.

Even today, forests, marshes, and meadows cover nearly one-eighth of the city. But it is not a safe haven for flowers and other herbaceous plants. Of 1,357 native plant species documented in New York City's history, only 778 remain there. There are various reasons for their disappearance—a pest we accidentally introduced, a habitat we made unwelcoming or destroyed—but always the causal factor is human. And our urban lives are impoverished in their absence.

Native plants continue to be pushed out of New York and other U.S. cities today. Forests are cut down to create ball fields, houses, and strip malls. Monocultures of turf lawn and impatiens lie in the places where biodiversity once flourished. Plants rarely figure into the land-use calculus when communities are searching for sites to establish parking lots, public works, and active recreational areas.

Imagine how much richer our daily lives would be if we began to notice and acknowledge the value of our natural environment. What if everyone learned how to identify ten wildflowers growing in their neighborhood? What if a city's annual budget accounted for ecosystem services like pollination and floodwater storage that came from the preservation of open space? This kind of ecological literacy could lead to protection of our threatened plant species and the conservation of our natural heritage for generations to come.

Here is a selection of native plants that have vanished from New York City. Some thrive elsewhere; others are barely hanging on. And one has recently reappeared in the city, a signal of hope in a concrete landscape.

This essay is adapted from an Op-Art feature originally published in the New York Times.

Large-Flowered Trillium | *Trillium grandiflorum*

If patience were to assume physical form, it would arrive as a large-flowered trillium. This plant's journey from seed to flower takes a long seven years. Then one spring, as we thrill to hear the robins call, the wait is over. The plant trumpets its arrival by carpeting the rich, moist forest floors it favors with its bright white blossoms. The beauty of this trillium is a detriment to its survival. People often pick the flowers, upsetting the slow-growing roots. Unscrupulous plant vendors dig whole plants from the wild and sell them on the cheap. This wildflower may wait as long as 20 years after a disturbance to resurface aboveground, as if to teach us a lesson. The last recorded sighting was in the 1990s in the Bronx.

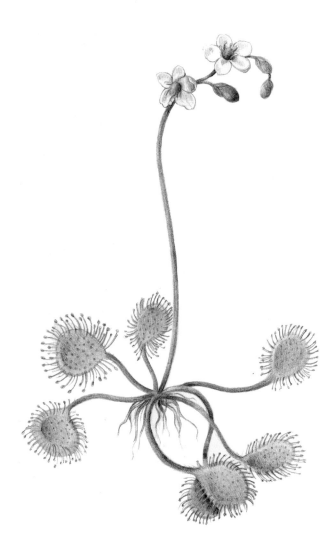

Round-Leafed Sundew | *Drosera rotundifolia*

Characterized by sandy, saturated soils, eastern U.S. coastal bogs are low-nutrient environments for plants. Round-leafed sundew compensates for this by practicing insectivory. Sticky glandular hairs on the edges and upper surfaces of the leaves enable the plant to attract, capture, and eat unsuspecting arthropod visitors. Insects become entangled in the leaf hairs, and triggered by movement, the leaf folds over, trapping the insect. The prey is then digested over the course of a week, providing vital nutrients to the plant. For all its evolutionary ingenuity, however, round-leafed sundew was unprepared for the loss of its habitat in New York City. It last grew in the bogs of coastal Brooklyn in 1952. Today, over 99 percent of the city's freshwater wetlands have been dredged, drained, or filled, leaving no room for such botanical marvels.

Hairy Lip Fern | *Cheilanthes lanosa*

Ferns are not flowering plants—evolutionarily, they are much older. Before angio-sperms and their attention-grabbing flowers came into the picture, ferns were ubiq-uitous. Up until recent times, ferns even flourished in Manhattan, where the rocky outcrops surfacing along the island's northern tip were excellent fern habitat. Hairy lip fern made its home there but was last recorded in 1866. It was most often seen nestled in clefts and nooks on the shady sides of exposed bedrock. Hairy lip fern sports a dense coat of spreading reddish hairs, so it would have given the rock surfaces in its upper Manhattan habitat a furry texture. This species is now absent from all of New York State; habitat destruction and air pollution are thought to have caused its downfall.

Eelgrass | *Zostera marina*

The shallow, subtidal waters off the shore of Manhattan were once filled with verdant life. Seagrass meadows flourished here and were dominated by eelgrass. The three-foot-long leaves of this submerged aquatic plant stretched and coiled with the tides while remaining firmly rooted in the substrate of the East River. The plant beds supported abundant wildlife, including numerous species of fish, and were food for waterfowl. Although eelgrass survived in Little Neck Bay in Queens as recently as 1987, it eventually succumbed—as did other New York City populations—to commercialization and pollution.

Rosepink | *Sabatia angularis*

This biennial wildflower produces dozens of blossoms and potentially thousands of seeds. The inviting pink flowers pop up in transitional moist meadows before woody plants grow up and cast too much shade. The species is ephemeral, with populations appearing, then quickly disappearing. It was thought to have completely vanished from New York City, but 11 years ago, rosepink was rediscovered in Staten Island on a sloping roadside. Instead of the turfgrass typically installed along highways, the natural vegetation and soils had been kept in place, offering a foothold for the plant. As in other urbanized areas around the country, houses, office buildings, strip malls, and sports fields have displaced most of New York City's native species. A few, like rosepink, are waiting for an opportunity to return.

Seasons of a Seed Collector

Heather Liljengren

It is mid-April, warm enough to layer up with just a sweatshirt. Rain is scheduled for the early afternoon, and it's finally one of the first full days of the field season. The red maples are starting to go to seed, and the first woodland wildflowers are beginning to bloom. I am visiting a park in the Bronx today. When you hear the words "park" and "the Bronx" mentioned in the same sentence, you may think of hot dogs and pinstripes at Yankee Stadium; but for me, they evoke thoughts of the rich, moist woodlands in Van Cortlandt Park, a thousand-acre green space and nature preserve in the northwestern corner of New York City.

I am on the hunt for a population of bloodroot (*Sanguinaria canadensis*), a native spring ephemeral. I'm optimistic because the previous summer I had found some remnant leaves of the plant in the woodlands. Until that discovery, I was aware of only a handful of confirmed populations within New York City. To find another would be very satisfying; to find it in seed, just before the pod splits and disperses all of it contents, would be a very good day at work.

A Basis for Restoration (Spring)

I am a seed collector, working at the New York City Department of Parks and Recreation's Greenbelt Native Plant Nursery, on Staten Island. It's my job to conservatively collect seed from naturally occurring, common native plants within the metropolitan region, as well as from species that are locally imperiled within the city limits. These seeds are then used to grow plants for restoration projects all over New York City. I travel throughout the five boroughs—Manhattan, the Bronx, Queens, Brooklyn, and Staten Island—as well as 19 other counties in New York State, New Jersey, and Connecticut looking for suitable plant populations. To help locate plants, I work closely with area botanists, study historical plant records, and research the habitat preferences of target species. Once I've identified wild populations, I receive permits for collection and follow very particular protocols. (Permits are required for anyone collecting on public lands.)

At the beginning of each field season, my colleagues and I develop a list of priority species to collect that year. The list is primarily determined by the needs of the many restoration projects our nursery has contracts for. To find suitable, healthy plant

Populations of the tiny, lovely bloodroot (*Sanguinaria canadensis*, seen here in spring flower) have grown rare in New York City.

populations, I scout city parks, county parks, state parks, and wildlife management areas. The goal for each outing is to collect at least 250 seeds of a targeted fern, grass, herb, shrub, or tree species. When I find a large enough population, I collect no more than 20 percent of the seed available on any particular collection day, in order to ensure that there's enough seed left to feed wildlife and recharge the natural seed bank.

At Van Cortland Park, I find the largest population of bloodroot that I have ever seen. It's a breathtaking sight: The plants cover a substantial portion of the forest floor, the scalloped green leaves hugging beautiful two-inch-wide white flowers with yellow stamens. They are spilling over sloping hills, peeking from behind the leaves of ramps, and finding their way through the encroaching multiflora rose (*Rosa multiflora*) and garlic mustard (*Alliaria petiolata*), two notorious exotic invaders. I stand between a highway and a golf course and marvel at how well this native plant is doing here.

More than 700 native plant species still naturally occur within the city limits. Some species, like *Sanguinaria canadensis*, are "exploitably vulnerable," meaning they're on the brink of becoming threatened, endangered, or extirpated within the state of New York. In New York City, habitat loss and fragmentation, soil compaction, air pollution, invasive plant species, and browsing by deer put constant pressure on native plant populations. An impressive number of natives, just like their human counterparts in the city, are tough and have adapted to deal with many of the harsh realities in the concrete jungle—but many other species need help.

Concerned citizens, restoration professionals, land managers, and landscapers can all play a part in preserving and rehabilitating these plants, and by doing so, support local biodiversity. As gardeners, we all can help by striving to re-create native habitat in our backyards, on our rooftops, and in vacant lots. Sustaining large populations of natives in parks and other remnant natural areas and preserves is also important. At Van Cortland Park, I pull up some garlic mustard and break off canes of multiflora rose that are crowding out the bloodroot.

Large, fleshy green seedpods are just starting to form on some of the plants. I'll return in about a month to see if the seeds are ready to collect, splitting open a pod and checking the color (*Sanguinaria* seeds typically turn a brownish red when mature) and also the hardness of individual seeds to see if the seed coats have toughened up. In addition, I'll perform a cut test to see if the embryos inside the seed are fully developed. I'll store the seedpods in a sealed plastic bag, as I do with all plants with fleshy fruit. This prevents the collection from drying out before I can get it back to the nursery. It's imperative to handle the collection properly, because every seed is potentially a new plant.

Knowing the Habitat of Your Plant (Early Summer)

Wild columbine (*Aquilegia canadensis*) has become one of my favorite early-summer collections. This plant is in high demand at Greenbelt Native Plant Nursery, and we have had to venture outside the five boroughs to find seed sources. Wild columbine had eluded me in my early days as a seed collector, but I was determined to find good, healthy populations. I researched the habitat that the plant favors—rocky hillsides, cliffs, and ridgetops—and went on numerous field trips. For a long time, I only managed to come across one or two plants, which wasn't going to cut it. When you collect seeds for conservation or restoration purposes, you want to capture as much genetic diversity as possible, and to do this, you need to sample from a population that consists of at least 50 individual plants. Moreover, taking seed from very small populations is just bad practice and not sustainable for the plants in their natural habitat. I needed to find an *Aquilegia* "city."

It is mid-June, and I'm driving back from an unsuccessful expedition to find a large enough population of azure bluet (*Houstonia caerulea*), those cute little white- to pale-blue-flowering perennials you sometimes spot on lawns before they're mowed. There are a few hours left in the day, and I decide to stop at Hamburg Wildlife Management Area in the highlands of New Jersey. I hike along an unfamiliar trail, an old riverbed, and begin surveying the rich moist woodlands around me. I continue to climb higher in elevation, picking the path that leads to dryer ground. To my left, I see some rocky edges deep off the trail and decide to check them out: Rocky areas in the highlands = cool plant species. I inspect the area, look down to get my footing, and there it is—the elusive *Aquilegia* nestled in the rocks.

My eyes search the immediate surroundings, and the plant keeps popping up around me. The finely divided green foliage looks almost blue against the gray cliffs. The best part is, the timing could not be better: Brown seed heads resembling fluted stars rise above all the thin stems. They are everywhere.

I look around, alone, yelling to myself, the plants, and the turkey vultures circling overhead, "This is amazing!" It's quite possible that I'm the only botanist who's ever come across this ridgeline and found these plants at the perfect time for seed collection. I feel giddy, cannot hold back the smile on my face, and make the best *Aquilegia* collection in the Greenbelt Native Plant Nursery's history. The seed heads are dry, so I put them in a breathable cheesecloth bag to prevent excess moisture from building up. I look into my full bag and experience the best natural high I have ever felt.

Bugs, Heat, and Other Obstacles (Late Summer)

Later that summer, as I scratch the oozing insect bites that cover my skin, my natural high has been replaced with a loathing I never knew I could have for a small creature. Chiggers have become my enemy, and I'm trying to figure out where they found me and climbed aboard. Was it in the meadow at the Great Swamp National Wildlife Refuge that I walked through collecting the Pennsylvania blackberry (*Rubus pensilvanicus*)? Or on the edge of the woodland at Willowbrook Park where I was crashing through common reeds (*Phragmites australis*), trying to find my truck?

Regardless, I know right away that I'm in for at least two weeks of agony. Chigger bites feel worse than poison ivy rash and mosquito bites combined. Hydrocortisone cream is the not-so-glamorous part of the job.

Dealing with bugs is just one of the many challenges of summer fieldwork. Thick, stifling heat is another: The middle of a swamp on a 90°F-plus day is unforgiving. The promise of eating fresh-picked wild blackberries or blueberries helps make it tolerable, as does the welcome reprieve of scouting near or in the water. Canoe collecting may be one of the best perks of this job. When you get to take a canoe to work, the discomfort of the sun and bites seems to fade away. Slowly traversing the water's edge in the Manasquan Reservoir, for example, you can reach that perfect seed or fruit cluster from an American hornbeam (*Carpinus caroliniana*) or a silky dogwood (*Cornus amomum*) that you could never get to if you stayed on land. Balancing in the canoe to reach branches becomes easier with practice; pushing the canoe out of the mud because you were too busy botanizing to notice that you were getting stranded can get a little tiresome.

Wherever you collect seed in the field, it's very important to be aware of your surroundings. In remote parts of city parks, I have come upon "wild" people who were not very happy that I found them. Once in a wildlife management area in the New Jersey highlands, I came upon a black bear and her three cubs who weren't so happy that I found them either. Every season has its obstacles, and each one of these affects how, when, and where seed collection is possible.

Importance of Local Adaptation (Fall)

Fall is a time of transition: Natural processes are slowing down, and all life is responding to the cooling temperatures and shortening length of the days. Birds and insects are preparing for the upcoming winter, and I am trying to beat the squirrels to the freshly fallen acorns. I never have enough hands or time to collect all the seed I'd like to. I just try to get to as many plants as I can before the propagules are dispersed.

It's the busiest time of year for me—the harvest season—and I collect seeds from a wide variety of habitats, from coastal salt marshes to highway medians. The importance of collecting local "ecotypic" seed is reaffirmed when I'm out in the field visiting these unique habitats. Native plants adapt over time to their immediate environmental conditions, leading to the formation of genetically distinct populations—or ecotypes—within individual species. It's a good strategy for restoration practitioners to use locally appropriate seeds and plants in their projects because these plants may be better equipped to survive. This may be doubly important in urban areas, where local conditions for plants and their pollinators can be very stressful and fragmented.

Perhaps native plants from tough natural habitats inside *and* outside the city can provide solutions for restoration in urban areas. When I'm on top of a ridgeline in the Palisades, for instance, I look around and see native plants adapted to shallow,

low-nutrient soils that would do well on a city green roof. When I visit our coastlines in Staten Island or Brooklyn and encounter native salt- and drought-tolerant plants, I envision them doing well in a street tree pit. Urban areas, with their many microclimates and habitat niches, could—with a little imagination—become opportunities for the preservation of native plants and the fauna they support.

The Rewards of Patience (Winter)

I love the stillness of the woods in the winter. It is late January, and I am bundled up to collect the berries of American holly (*Ilex opaca*). It has been one of the most amazing winter seasons, with enough snow in the metropolitan region that Vermonters are jealous. I'm patient as I make my way through three feet of snow on the forest floor in Monmouth County, New Jersey, just as the seeds of the *Ilex* are patient in their wait to germinate and produce new plants. *Ilex* seeds, like those of many northern U.S. native plants, must go through a long period of stratification (a dormancy roller coaster punctuated by alternating sustained cold weather and warm, moist summer conditions) before they will germinate. In the unique case of *Ilex*, it takes three to four years for seed dormancy to break. Each mature berry contains four to nine seeds, and each one of these will have to wait its turn before it's ready to leave the nursery as a young plant. We are all patient.

The use of native plants in restoration, design, and even agriculture has begun to gather momentum in recent years. It's taken a while for us to get to this point, but perhaps the idea of using natives has had—like the plants themselves—to "overwinter" in the minds of the large majority of growers, contractors, landscapers, and gardeners before it could germinate.

Every season that I am out in the field, I see more clearly the potential of native plant species to become horticultural gems that gardeners cannot live without. They may also be our best defense against the exotic invasive plant species that are claiming open spaces. I also see the man-made and environmental obstacles that many of these native plants face, from development to climate change. The choices that we make about what to grow and how to manage our lands will undoubtedly decide the fate of many native plant species.

As I hold the bag of freshly picked holly berries on this cold, beautiful day, I can only hope that my collecting efforts help return native plant species to places from which they have been removed.

Nibbling on Natives
Russ Cohen

Foraging for edible wild plants typically involves a considerable amount of effort. Every once in a while, though, you get a lucky break. That's what happened to me one spring when I was paddling the Contoocook River in central New Hampshire. A patch of groundnut (*Apios americana*), a native edible species, had made its home in the sandy soil along the river. The main edible portion of this plant—the tuberous roots—grow several inches underground, and harvesting them usually requires quite a bit of digging. But the Contoocook had flooded that spring, washing away a layer of topsoil and exposing the groundnut tubers. All I had to do was bend down and pick them up. Yum!

The groundnut is similar in flavor and texture to the potato and has its own storied past. It was once a major food resource for Native Americans and also became a staple for early European explorers and settlers in New England. (It was groundnut tubers, not corn, that kept the Pilgrims of Plymouth alive during the harsh winter of 1620–1621, their first in the New World.) While the aboveground part of the groundnut—a vine with compound, beanlike leaves and fragrant, chocolate-colored flowers—is herbaceous and dies back at the end of each growing season, the edible tubers are available year-round. A skillful forager can spot the dried vines and trace them to the tubers, even in the middle of winter.

That's what I did one year during a cross-country ski weekend in Vermont. The higher elevations were snow-covered, but in the warmer valley where I was staying, the ground wasn't yet frozen. I went for an early-morning walk along a nearby river and noticed the familiar-looking dried vines. I followed them along the ground, started digging, and sure enough, unearthed some sizable groundnut tubers. Later that morning, we cut the starchy tubers into thin slices, fried them in a little vegetable oil until golden, and ate them with our breakfast.

First Child in the Woods

Connecting to the landscape of the Northeast through my taste buds has been a passionate pursuit of mine for the last four decades. I grew up in the town of Weston, Massachusetts, a woodsy suburb west of Boston, where I had one of those quintessential "playing in the woods" childhoods extolled by psychologist Richard Louv in

A native in most parts of North America, grayleaf red raspberry (*Rubus idaeus* subsp. *strigosus*) is a familiar indigenous edible, offering tasty treats for forest foragers.

his seminal book, *Last Child in the Woods*. I fondly remember pushing rocks around in streams to create swimming holes and riding my one-speed, fat-tire Royce Union bicycle on trails in the surrounding woods well before "mountain biking" became popular. Other than the occasional family berry picking or nutting expedition, however, I didn't have much exposure to, nor was I particularly interested in, eating wild plants. I distinctly recall my father giving me one of Euell Gibbons's books on wild edibles (I think it was *Stalking the Wild Asparagus*) when I was in eighth grade, but I didn't even glance at it.

But two years later, my lifelong passion for foraging was sparked. I enrolled in a minicourse, Edible Botany, offered by the high school biology department, in which we learned about two dozen edible species that grew around the high school grounds. For the course's finale, my classmates and I prepared and shared dishes made from the plants we had learned about. That class got me so excited about foraging that I subsequently went to the town library and took out every book I could find on the topic. Over the next two years, I taught myself more than 50 more edible wild plant species, and in my senior year of high school, I taught a section of the Edible Botany class I had taken as a sophomore.

My enthusiasm for foraging—and teaching people about foraging—continues unabated to this day. I find that my connection with edible wild plants enriches my time spent outdoors, whether it be in a vacant lot near my office in downtown Boston, in the suburbs where I live, along the seacoast, or in the mountains. I spot edible wild plants just about everywhere I go. Even if I'm not actively hunting and gathering, just encountering an edible plant on a walk is like seeing an old friend coming to greet me along the way.

The Natives Versus Exotics Debate

Here is where I admit that I do not chant the "native species are good; nonnative species are bad" mantra as fervently as some native plant advocates. I enjoy finding and nibbling on exotics (including many weeds and invasive species) just as much as I do natives. I don't insist on checking a plant's passport or pedigree before deciding whether or not to eat it (though I do make sure it's not rare or endangered)—my main question is, "How yummy are you?" If the ecologists eradicate edible weeds and invasives from our landscape, so be it, but in the meantime, as long as these plants are here, I will pick and eat as many of them as I can, and encourage others to do so too.

As I see it, the very fact that many nonnative edible species maintain a pervasive presence in our midst while offering relatively few if any ecological benefits makes them ideal, "guilt-free" foraging targets. For example, of the 66 species featured in the Massachusetts Department of Fish and Game's booklet *A Guide to Invasive Plants in Massachusetts*, at least 20 are edible, including the delicious exotics autumn olive (*Elaeagnus umbellata*), black locust (*Robinia pseudoacacia*), common

A Note on Responsible Wild Harvesting

When foraging for natives, it's important to follow good conservation practices. Never harvest any plants that are rare, threatened, or endangered. (To check on the conservation status of a native plant, visit the USDA's PLANT Database, usda.plants.gov.) Only harvest from large populations of a species, and do so sparingly so that the plant will continue to thrive in that location. Berry picking and nut gathering are relatively benign foraging activities, because all you are doing is gathering the seed dispersal portion of the plant, and usually you will be able to find enough berries and nuts for yourself and still leave plenty behind for wildlife to eat. Digging up a plant or stripping its leaves are more disruptive foraging practices that could cause harm to native plant populations or habitats. Use these methods sparingly for common species and never for rare ones.

barberry (*Berberis vulgaris*), dame's rocket (*Hesperis matronalis*), Japanese knotweed (*Polygonum cuspidatum*), and wineberry (*Rubus phoenicolasius*). As far as most ecologists are concerned, they'd be thrilled if you and I picked and ate as many of these species as we possibly could, provided we don't help spread them around in the process, which is usually easy to avoid doing.

That said, some of my favorite edible plants are natives. Of the 42 plants featured in my foraging book *Wild Plants I Have Known...and Eaten* (Essex County Greenbelt Association, 2004), more than half are native to the Northeast, including sassafras (*Sassafras albidum*), groundnut, cattail (*Typha* species), serviceberry (*Amelanchier* species), common milkweed (*Asclepias syriaca*), pokeweed (*Phytolacca americana*), staghorn sumac (*Rhus typhina*), and shagbark hickory (*Carya ovata*). I also support the growing trend among homeowners and property managers to incorporate more native plant species into their landscaping.

Another Good Reason to Plant Natives

Natives are most often grown to attract wildlife, but some provide delicious treats for people too. Once you begin to explore the comestible charms of native plants, you'll find that many are at least as tasty as their domesticated or more familiar exotic counterparts, if not more so. (Compare the nuts of our native black walnut, *Juglans nigra*, with those of regular store-bought walnuts and you'll see what I mean.)

And in most cases, it should be possible for a native species planting to provide ample food for wildlife as well as people. For instance, most mature serviceberry plants are at least nine feet tall, which means their upper branches are out of human foragers' reach. We can content ourselves with the fruit from the lower branches, and all that fruit at the top is the songbirds' share.

I recently developed a version of my presentation on foraging that showcases only native edible species. My goal is to persuade gardeners not entirely sold on the idea of planting natives for their ecological or aesthetic benefits to "go native" because of how delicious some of these plants are to eat. For extra effect, I accompany my talk with a few tasty, wild-foraged treats made from native species. I know that my slide show is not going to convince everyone to rip up their lawns and put in edible native plants, but I'm optimistic that it will induce some folks still on the fence to give them a try.

A Sampling of Tasty Natives

Following are tidbits about some of our tastiest Northeast native plants.

Beach Plum
Prunus maritima

The location of wild populations of this prized native plum is often a heavily guarded secret among wild food foragers. What's more, the fruits, which ripen to a dull purple color around Labor Day, are hard to see except at close range. A good trick is to "pre-identify" the plant in the landscape when it's blooming in May: Masses of creamy-white flowers make beach plum bushes easy to spot from a distance. Beach plums (more the size of a cultivated cherry than a plum) can be quite tart, so they're mostly used for jam and other recipes that employ lots of sugar. But occasionally, you can find fruits that are quite sweet and delicious when eaten right off the bush. Beach plums are sometimes planted (and may even grow wild) many miles from the ocean, so keep on the lookout for them even where you might not otherwise expect to find them.

Black Walnut
Juglans nigra

The nuts of black walnut are often found in abundance along roadsides in early October. Wrapped up in their spicy-smelling green husks, they are similar in size and color to old tennis balls. Harvesting is simple enough: Remove the husks (an admittedly messy task) and allow the nuts (still in their shells) to dry out for at least several weeks. Then, use a hammer or vice to crack them open. Black walnuts have an assertive, aromatic flavor, quite different from that of store-bought walnuts (*Juglans regia*). The flavor works well in recipes that use honey as a sweetener (for baklava, for example). Before introducing this tree to your yard, though, beware that it will likely have an allelopathic (growth-inhibiting) effect on some plant species growing nearby.

Carrion Flower
Smilax herbacea

A thornless, nonwoody cousin of roundleaf greenbrier (*Smilax rotundifolia*, also edible), carrion flower sends up delicious young shoots that can be harvested and prepared in a similar manner to asparagus (a distant relative). Be sure to do your harvesting before the plant flowers in May and June. The blooming plant smells just like dirty gym socks or rotting meat and can be a bit off-putting. Nevertheless, some edible landscapers have chosen to deliberately introduce this plant to their yards in the hope that it will attract the carrion fly pollinators that some other native edible species, such as pawpaw (*Asimina triloba*), also rely upon.

Cattail
Typha latifolia and *T. angustifolia*

Dubbed by 1960s-era wild foods guru Euell Gibbons as the "supermarket of the swamps" because of its many edible portions—including the rhizomes, sprouts, hearts, and immature flower spikes—cattail has a mild flavor reminiscent of artichoke and cucumber. Even the (hypoallergenic) pollen can be collected and added to flour to make attractive and nutritious baked products such as crepes and muffins. If this wetland landscaping choice is too bland for you, consider the spicier sweet flag (*Acorus calamus*), a plant with similar habitat preferences. Sweet flag rhizomes were once candied and eaten as an after-dinner treat. My favorite part is the tender, yellowish foliage in the center of the growing plant that adds a spicy, ginger-like flavor when used in salads.

Evening Primrose
Oenothera biennis

Though it favors fields, disturbed ground, and forest-edge habitats like many of our exotic weeds, evening primrose is indeed a native species. The main edible part of this biennial species is the taproot. Resembling a small parsnip in flavor and size but with some pink coloration at the crown, it is at its best for eating from the end of the first growing season to the beginning of the second (October to April). The root is tasty grated and substituted for the potato in potato pancake recipes.

Restoring Native Communities
Myla Aronson

It's 8 a.m. and already 85°F—August on Long Island. Three undergraduate students, one high school student, and I are measuring the growth of prairie plants in a vacant lot in Uniondale, New York, in the heart of the nation's original suburbia. We're surrounded by four-foot-tall flowering stems of purpletop tridens (*Tridens flavus*), little yellow flowers of slender goldentop (*Euthamia caroliniana*), and happy-looking orange flowers of butterfly milkweed (*Asclepias tuberosa*). Even after just two months, this restoration is already starting to look like a prairie. Local residents and college students drive by and stare. Some honk. Others want to know what vegetables we are growing. "Any tomatoes?" they ask.

When you think Long Island, prairie is probably not the first thing that pops into your head. Instead, the word conjures images of 1950s-style suburban tract housing and Gatsbyesque Gold Coast mansions. Not to mention population density: Nassau County, which is near the western tip of Long Island and includes the town of Uniondale, had a population of 1,339,532 in 2010. That's 4,672 people per square mile, one of the highest concentrations of people in the country.

What most people do not know is that Nassau County is also home to one of the only true prairie ecosystems on the east coast of the U.S.—the Hempstead Plains. Growing on a vast area of flat land produced by outwash from the Wisconsin Glaciation, 10,000 to 12,000 years ago, the plains once covered an estimated 30,000 to 60,000 acres. Today, there are only a few small remnants left—the largest of which is a 19-acre site next to Nassau Community College, managed by the Friends of Hempstead Plains, a local conservation group. The vacant lot we're working on is only a quarter acre in size and is flanked by housing on three sides and a parking lot across the street. My research is investigating whether or not it's possible to restore a native plant community—such as a prairie—in a landscape that's as built up and fragmented as suburban Long Island.

Long Island's Lost Prairie
When you walk through the 19-acre Hempstead Plains remnant and close your mind to the cars whizzing by on the adjacent Meadowbrook Parkway, you feel as if you were in a tallgrass prairie in Iowa or Minnesota. You even half expect to see buffalo

When the native grasses, thoroughworts, and goldenrods of Long Island's Hempstead Plains prairie remnant bloom in fall, the display is spectacular.

grazing in the distance. In 1991, biologist Richard Stalter and colleagues compared the plant community in the remnant with that of the Konza Prairie, in Kansas, and found many similar species. Despite its small size, the fragment retains the essential composition and complexity of a true prairie.

The destruction of the Hempstead Plains was gradual, stretching back two centuries or more. During the late 18th and 19th centuries, many acres were used as training grounds for soldiers. Early in the 20th century, the level landscape of the prairie, dominated by grasses and forbs (broad-leafed herbs), was found to be a perfect landing field for aircraft. The grassy runways were maintained with little management, and planes parked amid birdfoot violet (*Viola pedata*), Nassau County's official flower, which carpeted the prairie with deep violet and lavender blossoms in the spring. By 1910 the area was home to a number of airfields, including what became Roosevelt field, America's busiest civilian airfield in the 1930s. Charles Lindberg took off from here in 1927 in the *Spirit of St. Louis* on his historic nonstop flight to France. Harriet Quimby, the first woman to fly across the English Channel, and later Amelia Earhart, spent sunny days here piloting their aircraft and breaking gender barriers.

The plains were also home to Mitchel Air Force Base, a crucial military defense and staging site active until 1961. Eventually the developers moved in, attracted by the same flat landscape that had drawn the pilots. They built roads, houses, shopping malls, and more, replacing the tranquil grasslands with suburban sprawl. Tens of thousands of acres of prairie were lost.

The Hempstead Plains habitat is ranked as critically imperiled—at very high risk of disappearing due to its extreme rarity at the state and global levels. Notable rare species include the federally endangered sandplain gerardia (*Agalinis acuta*), an annual with small purplish-pink flowers; the birdfoot violet; and the yellow-flowered bushy rockrose (*Helianthemum dumosum*). Grasses, milkweeds, and goldenrods form the basis of a diverse vegetation mosaic (featuring 250 different species) that sustains birds, butterflies, and other animals. When they bloom in fall, the display is quite spectacular.

The plains are now protected from further development, but other agents of destruction threaten what remains of this unique landscape. These include encroachment by woody plants, due to the suppression of wildfires, which historically kept colonizing trees and shrubs at bay. Nonnative invasive species such as Russian olive (*Elaeagnus angustifolia*), cypress spurge (*Euphorbia cyparissias*), and Chinese lespedeza (*Lespedeza cuneata*) are also wreaking havoc on the native grassland community.

Ecological Restoration 101

The vacant lot in Uniondale where I've sited my restoration project is owned by Hofstra University, my employer. I've given it the fancy name the Hofstra University Suburban Ecological Research Site (HUSERS); my students prefer to call it "the field plot." I made the choice to restore the Hempstead Plains ecosystem here because that

A Restoration Success Story

Sandplain gerardia (*Agalinis acuta*, right) is a small annual related to snapdragons that grows in coastal grasslands along the mid Atlantic. Designated endangered by the U.S. Fish and Wildlife Service, one of its few significant populations is found in the Hempstead Plains on Long Island, New York. The species requires a high-quality native grassland dominated by little bluestem (*Schizachyrium scoparium*) to grow; scientists believe it gets its nutrients and moisture from bluestem's roots in a sort of parasitic relationship. Growing the species in greenhouses has not been effective.

Thirty years ago, the sandplain gerardia was all but wiped out along with its prairie habitat. Its habitat has been lost not just to intensive development but also due to the suppression of wildfires and suspension of cultural practices like grazing that in the past kept the grasslands from being invaded by weeds and shrubs.

While groups like the Friends of Hempstead Plains (friendsofhp.org) have championed the preservation of our last prairie remnants, conservationists have worked to increase plant populations. Mature seeds of sandplain gerardia are collected by hand and sown in areas of likely habitat. As a result of careful stewardship, on Long Island the total numbers of the plant have increased from a few hundred in 1990 to thousands today.

was the original, pre-Columbian ecosystem of this plot of land—and it's standard practice in restoration ecology to attempt to reestablish the historical trajectory of a disturbed or degraded site.

When designing a restoration, even a restoration experiment, you must first identify the sources of disturbance, or "drivers of change" in the degraded site. Sometimes it's possible to restore an ecosystem simply by removing one or more of these drivers and allowing for an independent recovery of that system. For example, when overabundant deer are removed from a forest ecosystem, seedlings and saplings of canopy trees regenerate by themselves.

In the case of the Hempstead Plains, the main driver of change is habitat destruction in the form of suburban development. This driver is impossible to reverse: The plants are gone, the soil has been degraded, the seed bank has been destroyed, and the houses, roads, schools, and malls that cover the original prairie are not going anywhere soon. Complicating matters more, the landscape is densely developed. This is not your standard American suburbia, with large lots and backyards that could potentially be used to create green corridors linking together nature preserves. The remnant parcels of the Hempstead Plains are isolated from each other by an unfriendly matrix of parking lots, hotels, college campuses, dense residential development, and of course, parkways.

So even when a disturbance is partially removed—in the case of HUSERS, the house occupying the site was demolished the year before the project was established—there is still no effective way for the prairie to regenerate by itself: No prairie seed in the ground; no prairie seed being carried in from the outside by wind or animal dispersers. The closest sources of little bluestem (*Schizachyrium scoparium*) and butterfly milkweed are 1½ miles away, at the 19-acre remnant of the Hempstead Plains at Nassau Community College. From the beginning of this project, it was clear that the "if you build it, they will come" approach wouldn't work, and that my students and I would have to employ the second main strategy of restoration ecology: deliberate reintroduction of native plants.

Shortly after the demolition of the house at HUSERS, cosmopolitan weeds and invasives moved in: crabgrass, dandelions, horseweed, mugwort, and Norway maple. (It was easy for these plants to disperse within the site because they were growing all over the neighborhood.) The first order of business was to mow the weeds and till the "soil," if you could call it that. Consisting mainly of fill from an unknown source, it was a nutrient-poor mix of sandy clay loam, rocks, and concrete debris, from which we plucked the occasional plastic pipe and lots of trash paper, Axe Body Wash bottles, a surprising number of pens and pencils, and cigarette butts. There was very little naturally occurring organic matter. The groundskeepers from Hofstra, who tilled the soil, kept trying to persuade me to add soil amendments, such as mulch or manure, but I insisted this "soil" was part of the experiment. (Why use pricey amendments if the plants will end up restoring the soil all by themselves?)

"Nothing will grow here," they said.

"We'll see," I replied.

The Plots Thicken

In June of 2010, my students and I planted 1,248 individual plants representing 12 species (6 grasses and 6 forbs common to the Hempstead Plains). All the plants were grown by the Long Island Native Plant Initiative—an amalgam of local nonprofits, government agencies, and nursery professionals dedicated to providing locally sourced natives—from local seed, mostly collected at Hempstead Plains remnants. We broke up the site into 52 one-by-one-meter plots, and planted 24 plants in each. I designed two treatments: Plots were planted either with all 12 species or with just 4 species (a random selection of 2 grasses and 2 forbs). I designed the experiment in this way to answer a number of different questions, such as "Which particular species will do best in this urban soil?" (always a good thing to know if you want your restoration to succeed).

Preliminary data collected after the first growing season indicate that many of the species are doing well, although some are performing better than others. Wild indigo (*Baptisia tinctoria*) has not survived well. The compacted soils and resulting lack of water appeared to bother this species in particular. Butterfly milkweed also did not thrive as well as other species, but those individuals that did survive produced beautiful orange flowers in early fall. Of the grasses, most flowered, and in fall, the seed heads of purpletop tridens were spectacular. Broom-sedge (*Andropogon virginicus*), a common species in the remnants, did not flower or even grow very much. When the plants died back in the fall, they added a vital first layer of organic matter to the soil, kick-starting the process of soil restoration.

In this project, I am asking many questions beyond the core one of how to restore native communities in a highly urbanized landscape. For instance, does native biodiversity reduce the impact of invasive species on a site, and if so, how much? It is often hypothesized that areas with more species (higher diversity) are more resistant to nonnative species invasions. Because of the way I designed the experiment, I'll be able to examine whether or not this holds true in a highly suburbanized landscape such as Uniondale. Gathering this data may help other prairie restoration practitioners reduce the damage caused by invasives on their sites.

Another question is whether or not a small, restored prairie functions in similar ways to a larger, original prairie. We know it will never attract nesting grasshopper sparrows—it's just too small. But we've seen in one growing season that many of the plants will grow, flower, and reproduce successfully, which implies that pollination is occurring. Pollination—essential to the continual success of plants in restored habitats—is an ecosystem service rarely studied in ecological restorations, so this year (2011) my students are investigating the pollination and reproductive success of early goldenrod (*Solidago juncea*) and butterfly milkweed and comparing populations of these species in the restored site with those in the 19-acre remnant "reference site." They are also examining whether or not the plants in the restored site attract the same pollinators as those in the reference site.

Is there value in establishing isolated restored native communities? I believe so. Only time will tell if the plant community we've established at HUSERS is a functioning one that can persist on its own with minimal human intervention. Hopefully it will attract birds, bees, and butterflies and lead to restoration of the soil food web. My students and I will continue to study the ecological dynamics of the restoration and compare them with those of the remnant site 1½ miles north. Most of all, I hope this little prairie in the 'burbs will show folks what biodiversity should look like in their area—and get them interested in the beautiful sea of grass and flowers that once covered the land where their streets and parking lots now lie. Already we are demonstrating that tomatoes aren't the only plants worth tending in a city lot. To children and adults who live in this dense suburban area and have limited exposure to nature, this place, and places like it, will surely matter.

The Future of My Forest

Bernd Heinrich

Compared with forests in many other parts of the country, those in Maine are doing quite well. Unlike elsewhere, our forests aren't being devastated by pests, diseases, drought, extreme wildfires, and other scourges, at least not yet. Here, forest can sometimes seem like a slowly rising tide, engulfing everything in its path. About 90 percent of the state's total land area, or 17.7 million acres, is forested. On my 600-acre property, I have to work hard to maintain a 1-acre area free of trees around my cabin. Every young red maple (*Acer rubrum*) I snip off sends up a dozen shoots the following year. A black locust (*Robinia pseudoacacia*) that I planted for sentimental reasons constantly sends out runners, and little black locust trees are coming up by the dozens all over the clearing. It's a constant battle to maintain any open space at all.

Then again, one man's "open space" is another man's jungle. My clearing is densely overgrown with meadowsweet, winterberry, blackberry, raspberry, and blueberry bushes, along with patches of fireweed and some grass, moss, forbs, and ferns. In the summer the place swarms with insects, especially bumble bees. The wild blueberries (*Vaccinium* species) and waist-high spirea bushes (*Spiraea* species), along with shoulder-high fireweed (*Chamerion angustifolium*), provide a haven for many wasps that parasitize forest insects and wild bees that pollinate flowers far and wide in the surrounding forest.

I try to preserve the open area and arrest the natural course of forest succession in order to nurture sun-loving plants and the animals they support. And I see this as part of the biodiversity of the forest—a diversity once maintained throughout the Northeast by fires, both naturally occurring and purposely set by Native Americans, but made possible in our era of fire suppression by surrogates such as cutting and pruning. (Note: Removing wood doesn't fill all the roles played by fire. For example, it doesn't help serotinous plants, such as certain pine species, that depend on heat from fire for seed release or germination.)

My clearing is a place where birds nest on or closely above the ground, and where they find a bonanza of insects and berries. I can usually spot a pair each of chestnut-sided warblers, Nashville warblers, robins, white-throated sparrows, cedar waxwings, goldfinches, tree swallows (in my bird boxes), phoebes (on my

Most woodlands of the eastern U.S. have regrown from land cleared for economic or agricultural uses a century ago. Careful stewardship can help maintain their biodiversity.

cabin), and yellowthroat warblers. Lately, a turkey has been nesting here as well. But what I most enjoy about this part of my forest is that it's the only available venue for the sky-dancing courtship displays of woodcocks, which nest and rear their young in the woods.

The forest surrounding this spot is regrowth from what used to be hayfields, apple orchards, and sheep and cattle pastures. Now, after over a hundred years, you couldn't tell it had ever been anything but woodland unless you knew what a "virgin" forest from this region looked like. A few years back, on a patch of adjacent property, I saw a sample: It was a beautiful sight, featuring sugar maple (*Acer saccharum*) and red maple trees over five feet thick at the breast height, as well as white ash (*Fraxinus americana*), American beech (*Fagus grandifolia*), red oak (*Quercus rubra*), and great red spruce (*Picea rubens*) scattered throughout. There were not only standing trees but also trees in all stages of decay on the ground. And the understory was open, except where a tree had recently fallen and young trees and other plants were competing for the light that fell to the floor in its absence.

But not long after, the patch was harvested in an absolute clear-cut—one in which not only the biggest and the best trees were taken (which might have been bearable) but all the rest too. Still, the forest will grow back, in one form or another.

A Mosaic of Vegetation

My forest stretches from a brook called Alder Stream, in a small valley, to the top of York Hill, hundreds of feet higher. Near the bottom of the property by the brook, there's a grassy area with a few tamaracks (*Larix laricina*). These grade into thickets of speckled alder (*Alnus incana* subsp. *rugosa*), which in turn grade into areas colonized by balsam fir (*Abies balsamea*). As you go higher, red maple, and first green ash (*Fraxinus pennsylvanica*) and then white ash fill in, along with white cedar (*Thuja occidentalis*). Above that, there are increasingly more hardwoods, such as yellow birch (*Betula alleghaniensis*) and paper birch (*B. papyrifera*), black cherry (*Prunus serotina*), and sugar maple. As you reach the top of the hill, red spruce becomes increasingly dominant.

In addition to this altitudinal pattern in the vegetation are two others. The first is a very local patchiness created by chance and circumstance. For instance, a fallen log among the hardwoods grows a layer of moss, and yellow birch seedlings have sprouted up there, having escaped being smothered by the large leaves that rain down from the canopy and cover the forest floor like a blanket every fall. A hummock above the permanently soaked soils in the alder bog has provided a foothold for a white birch, a red maple, and some firs.

The second pattern is the historic imprint. One area on the property was burned, possibly by a natural wildfire, a century or more ago, which provided ideal habitat for the rapid colonization of balsam fir, poplar, and spruce. Another is a former pasture in which stood an old white pine (*Pinus strobus*) that seeded in and produced offspring that outgrew their competitors and have now become giants. The old apple orchard had sugar maples bordering it, and one year when they flowered (most years they don't), they showered the ground with seeds, which subsequently germinated and grew because they had a head start on the balsam firs that usually sprout.

Selective Cutting

My forest grows trees well, and I have enrolled it in Maine's Tree Growth Tax Program, which helps ease my tax burden. "Tree growth" designation means not so much that I grow trees (they grow anyway), but that I harvest them. I have no problem with that, because I believe that through my selective cutting, I now have a more diverse, healthy forest than the one I started with over 30 years ago.

The local loggers who've cut on my property have varied in their methods, from the man with a chainsaw and skidder (a heavy vehicle used for dragging logs away from a cutting site) to the horse logger with a team of Percheron draft horses, to the logger with an industrial feller buncher (a large motorized tree harvester). I can't say that I have a blanket preference for one method over another; each one has its pros and cons. For instance, the horse logger left a very minor local imprint at the sites where he cut down trees but ultimately a much larger one than the other two: You can't ask a horse to drag each and every log a mile or more—so the horse logger needed to make a road in so a truck could haul out what he had cut.

All logging operations involve the use of a landing, a staging area where the wood is brought before being hauled off by trucks. A log landing can look like a moonscape once the work has stopped, but within several years, it became a woodcock display area, and now 15 years after that, my landing has become a bird hot spot and moose pasture and is one of my favorite sites to visit in the forest. Grasses seeded in, then raspberries and cherries, and I sprinkled some acorns around. Besides the clearing around the cabin, it's the only place on my property where mourning warblers nest.

Striving for Diversity

One patch of my forest lies on a west-sloping hillside that was a sheep pasture about 200 years ago. In 1974, when I bought the property, this area was a dark, wildlife-unfriendly thicket of balsam firs with some pines and hardwoods sprinkled in. In the late 1980s, I asked my neighbor Dalton Procter, who owns a skidder and does some logging on the side, to "make some light" in there. He took most of the fir, leaving at my request the already large and rapidly growing pines.

Those pines are now giants. In between them a thicket of striped maple (*Acer pensylvanicum*) and other hardwoods have sprung up. The moose and deer have found much winter browse here, and now new young pine, beech, oak, spruce, and fir are shooting up. Like in an economy, a diverse forest is a healthy forest, and a healthy forest ecosystem has young and adult trees, as well as snags, or standing dead trees, and wood on the ground in various states of decay. The area has no resemblance to the uninviting, even-aged fir thicket that it was not long ago.

As a private, residential landowner, I know every hillside, every patch of fir and spruce, and I know what grows where and how fast. It's not in my interest to abuse my forest the way the big companies do—creating clear-cuts in order to have a uniform monoculture of tree stands, turning my backyard into chemical-dependent agricultural fields, where pesticides and herbicides are applied to "rescue" the trees and maintain the plantations.

I have given some thought to the future of my forest, and perhaps by extension, to others. Every patch within my forest is so different that it has taught me to be careful about extrapolating from one forest to another; but nonetheless, some fundamental strategies, such as maintaining diversity, seem to apply. Diversity not only creates visual interest and habitat opportunities but also is linked to resilience—the ability of an ecosystem to withstand and recover from disturbance—and may be key to preserving the long-term integrity of the forest in the face of potential perils such as pests, diseases, and climate change. These threats vary in different forests depending on geography, site conditions, and land-use history; however, with diversity comes redundancy, so that if one group of plants founders (for example, the ashes), another will be present to take its place.

So far, the forests of Maine—including my own forest—have not been as seriously impacted by insect pests, fungal diseases, and invasive exotic plants as other forests in the U.S., in part because of the state's history of low-intensity development. (The chestnut blight is one obvious exception—the fungus has killed most American chestnut trees in Maine.) But the threats are mounting. Hemlock woolly adelgid is established in southern coastal areas of Maine, and garlic mustard (*Alliaria petiolata*) and Japanese barberry (*Berberis thunbergii*) are also gaining a foothold in the state. As I'm writing this, the emerald ash borer has been identified 140 miles from Maine's western border in Quebec Province (transportation of firewood from out of state into Maine has been banned in an effort to prevent the spread of the borer).

We must do what we can to prevent the introduction and advance of these pests, and to mitigate other threats to the long-term health of our native trees. But we also need truly sustainable forestry that preserves biological diversity and maintains the ecological function of our productive forests—forestry that prioritizes the long-term stewardship and health of our native trees and the animals they support.

Major Threats to Native Forests

Niall Dunne

Following are short profiles of some of the major disease organisms and invasive species undermining the health of our forests. Researchers and government officials are working hard to limit the spread of these pests by developing control methods and imposing quarantines on infested areas.

Asian longhorned beetle

Asian Longhorned Beetle First detected in New York City in 1996, this large, shiny black and white exotic beetle is attacking and killing a wide range of trees, predominantly maples, in some urban areas in New York, Illinois, New Jersey, Massachusetts, and Ohio.

Emerald Ash Borer This metallic green Asian beetle was first discovered in the U.S. in 2002 in the state of Michigan, having most likely entered the country in solid wood packing material. It has since killed tens of millions of native ash trees in the Northeast and Midwest.

Garlic Mustard Introduced from Europe as a winter potherb in colonial times, this cool-season biennial is wreaking havoc on sugar maple forests and floodplain environments in most eastern and midwestern states and the Pacific Northwest. A prolific seeder with no natural enemies in the U.S., it is gradually displacing many native woodland wildflower populations.

Hemlock Woolly Adelgid First detected in Virginia in 1951, this small, aphidlike insect from Asia presents a major threat to eastern hemlock (*Tsuga canadensis*) and Carolina hemlock (*T. caroliniana*) in the eastern U.S. It has already killed large numbers of hemlocks in parts of Virginia, New Jersey, Pennsylvania, and Connecticut.

Mountain Pine Beetle This small black native bark beetle is attacking a range of pine (*Pinus*) species in much of western North America in what may be the largest insect pest outbreak ever recorded. Climate change is contributing to the severity of the outbreak by expanding the beetle's range.

Sudden Oak Death Caused by the water mold *Phytophthora ramorum*, this disease has killed hundreds of thousands of tanoaks (*Lithocarpus densiflorus*) and susceptible oak (*Quercus*) species in the California coastal region and southwestern Oregon since it was first reported in 1995. Nonfatal infections of foliar hosts such as camellias and rhododendrons are helping to spread the disease.

For detailed information on these and other forest threats, visit the APHIS Plant Health website, www.aphis.usda.gov/plant_health/plant_pest_info/.

Conservation in the Age of Climate Change

Janet Marinelli

"Bring lots of water!" warned Gil Nelson, an expert on the flora of the Florida Panhandle, as we prepared for a hike in Torreya State Park, which in late July can be stupefyingly hot. Nelson, a tall man with a beard, the badge of honor for so many botanists, donned a wide-brimmed straw hat. Pam and Bill Anderson, who live on the edge of the park, handed out carved walking sticks, essential equipment for traversing the forests that clutch the sharp-sloped ravines, called steepheads, along a short stretch of the upper Apalachicola River. Bill Anderson carried the most important piece of paraphernalia, a handheld GPS device he has been using since 2003 to document every Florida torreya tree (*Torreya taxifolia*) he and Pam encounter during their many rambles in the region.

We clambered down a precipitous trail from sun-bleached, logging-pocked pinelands into a humid, dark, almost otherworldly steephead forest. Dainty maidenhair fern (*Adiantum capillus-veneris*) and white doll's-eyes (*Actaea pachypoda*) luxuriated in the dense shade cast by an astonishing assortment of trees and shrubs—oak-leaf hydrangea (*Hydrangea quercifolia*), leatherwood (*Cyrilla racemiflora*), Florida yew (*Taxus floridana*), overtopped by massive southern magnolias (*Magnolia grandiflora*) and muscular American beeches (*Fagus grandifolia*), to name but a few. In places, the nearly two-foot-long leaves of the rare Ashe's magnolia (*M. macrophylla* subsp. *ashei*) rose above a skirt of flame azalea (*Rhododendron calendulaceum*), whose bright yellow-orange blooms perfume the air with sweet honeysuckle scent in spring. In a vast biotic convergence, species from the Gulf and Atlantic coastal plains merge here, while subtropical plants mingle with northern denizens driven south over eons by glaciers.

Only our footsteps broke the stillness as we crunched through the thick litter of leathery magnolia leaves, zigzagging around golden orb spider webs draped among the trees. Nelson pointed out that 100 of the plant species found here grow nowhere else in Florida, and nearly a dozen, like the Florida torreya, occur nowhere else in the world.

Several times during the Pleistocene, the period that spanned the planet's most recent glacial episodes, most of Florida was the bottom of an ancient sea. When the

The critically endangered Florida torreya is poised on the brink of extinction; only the occasional struggling sapling remains in the wild.

climate warmed, the massive glaciers to the north melted and the sea swelled, leaving only a narrow strip of northern Florida. When the climate cooled, the glaciers grew and the sea retreated, leaving shorelines of limestone and sand, into which millennia of rainfall and sapping erosion have etched the Apalachicola's steepheads. Some plunge at inclines close to 45 degrees—enough to induce wooziness in Floridians accustomed to pancake-flat terrain.

The primeval vegetation and antediluvian past of the Apalachicola's lush ravines led some old-timers to conclude that the area was the site of the Garden of Eden. They also believed the gopher wood tree, found only in the region, to be the gopher wood the Bible says Noah used to build his ark. As glaciers melt and the sea swells anew, the tree, known more commonly today as the Florida torreya, no longer casts an evergreen veil over the Apalachicola's steep slopes. The fossil record indicates that this member of the yew family, with its sharply pointed needles and a classic Christmas tree shape, is one of the older extant tree species on earth and was once among the area's most abundant trees, with a total estimated population surpassing 600,000. Today, the Florida torreya is poised on the brink of extinction. Decimated by a combination of causes, including overcutting and disease, it no longer survives aboveground long enough to reproduce in the wild. Only the occasional struggling sapling remains, sprouting from old roots.

A New Threat

Climate change may be hastening the Florida torreya's demise. It is widely believed that the conifer is a cool-climate species that once grew in the Appalachians. Pushed southward to the Florida Panhandle during the ice ages, it was unable to reclaim its original northern habitats when the ice sheets retreated.

The Florida torreya is far from alone. In its 2006 "Declaration on Climate Change and Plant Conservation," the Gran Canaria Group, comprised of botanic gardens and other conservation groups around the world, calculates that as many as half of the estimated 400,000 plant species in existence today may be facing extinction in the 21st century. This is staggering news for plant conservationists, whose work is already made difficult by the rapid destruction of habitat and its invasion by aggressive nonnative species. Climate change is forcing them to reexamine even the most basic assumptions: How do you define "native" as plants from the south move northward into a region? What is a "natural community"? And how do you decide which plants deserve protection?

The iconic American landscape of Concord, Massachusetts, is already feeling the effects of global warming. Around 150 years ago, Henry David Thoreau spent hours each day traversing Concord's fields and forests observing nature. He had a special interest in flowers, especially when they first bloomed in spring. Before he died in 1862 at the age of 44, Thoreau compiled charts listing the first flowering dates for several hundred species.

For three years beginning in 2003, Boston University biologist Richard Primack and postdoctoral researcher Abraham Miller-Rushing retraced Thoreau's footsteps to determine how the birches (*Betula*), blueberries (*Vaccinium*), and goldenrods (*Solidago*) and other wildflowers of the Concord landscapes once frequented by the famous naturalist have been faring. They found only about 400 of the 600 plant species in Thoreau's charts. They ascertained that from 1852 to 2006, due to urbanization and climate change, Concord has warmed 4.3 degrees Fahrenheit, and as a result, some common plants such as highbush blueberry (*V. corymbosum*) are flowering at least three weeks earlier than in Thoreau's day. On average, spring flowers in Concord are blooming a full seven days earlier than in the 1850s.

Globally, according to the Intergovernmental Panel on Climate Change, the earth's mean surface temperature has already warmed, on average, more than 1 degree Fahrenheit over the last century, and depending on factors such as how successful we are at curbing greenhouse gas emissions, temperatures could climb another 2 to 11.5 degrees by the end of this century. (To put things in perspective, it is 9 degrees warmer now than it was during the last ice age.) As a result, plants are flowering earlier, not just in Concord but around the world.

Plants are also responding to climate change by shifting their ranges toward the poles and up mountainsides. In 1994, after surveying 26 summits in the Alps, Austrian researchers published the first comprehensive study to document such wholesale movement of plants. They found species had migrated skyward at a rate of about 3 feet a decade in the 20th century, with some moving 12 feet in a decade.

Rooted in place, the vast majority of plants have not evolved for rapid locomotion, and their seeds typically disperse a few hundred yards at most. "Some weedy species will probably be able to adapt in place to climate change—that's why they're weeds. But other plants probably will not," says Kay Havens, director of plant sciences and conservation at the Chicago Botanic Garden. During past episodes of climate change, many plants were able to keep pace with the changes. As glaciers waxed during the Pleistocene, for example, some plants of the eastern forests survived by migrating south to so-called refugia like the upper Apalachicola, which is one reason why the area is a pocket of dazzling diversity even today.

Studies of the migration of species like the American beech and red maple (*Acer rubrum*) during the last glacial period suggest they were an order of magnitude slower than those required for the current rate of climate change. A research paper published in 2009 in the science journal *Nature* predicts that mean temperatures will shift rapidly toward the poles, about a third of a mile per year, on average, in the 21st century. The velocity of climate change will vary by location, depending on such factors as latitude and topography. It will be fastest—about three quarters of a mile per year—over flat areas like marshes, mangrove swamps, and deserts. In the most extreme scenarios, it could be as much as six miles per year. Without human help, countless species may not be able to migrate fast enough, and others will be stopped dead in their tracks by housing subdivisions, shopping malls, and sprawling industrial complexes.

Severe droughts, increasing wildfires, fierce storms, and rising seas are among the better-known consequences of the global climate changes already under way. But few people are aware that once-familiar landscapes are already in flux and are likely to change drastically during the decades to come. Plants and the animals that depend on them, all moving at their own rate, will find themselves with implausible companions in novel ecosystems. In a hundred years, for example, California's Central Valley could become the preferred habitat for many cacti and succulents now found in Arizona. Along the coast, California's iconic redwoods (*Sequoia sempervirens*) could still be hanging on because adult trees are so long-lived, but the climate will have become so dry and inhospitable to young trees that the adults will be a forest of the living dead, unable to reproduce. Scientists have only recently begun to grapple with this prospect of a not-too-distant future when there may be no redwoods in California, no torreya trees in Florida, no sugar maples (*Acer saccharum*) in Vermont.

Changing Conservation Strategies

"Careful—they bite!" quips Ron Determann as he shows off a Florida torreya branch covered with its signature prickly needles, along with the rounded, bluish-green cones that have become so rare. The future of this species and other imperiled plants now lies in the capable hands of horticulturists like this unassuming man, the director of the Atlanta Botanical Garden's spectacular conservatory complex. He's one of a mere handful of people who have managed to coax this plant, which no longer lives long enough to produce seed in the wild, to produce it in cultivation. In fact, Determann and his crew have propagated more than 1,000 torreya trees—which may be more than survive in the wild along the Appalachicola. The reputed gopher wood of Noah's ark may one day endure only in a modern-day ark of conservationsts' pots and propagation beds.

As part of the Center for Plant Conservation, the Atlanta Botanical Garden works with other conservation groups and government agencies to save at-risk species like the Florida torreya. "The idea is to create a backup system" for the species by propagating plants, says Jenny Cruse Sanders, the garden's director of conservation and research.

Until recently, conservationists were pursuing a strategy devised before the implications of climate change became apparent. They established a network of preserves and other protected areas. They did what they could to halt the spread of invasive, nonnative species that are making these habitats less hospitable for native plants and animals. They brought rare plants like the Florida torreya into cultivation and bolstered remaining populations by returning propagated plants to their native range in the wild.

This strategy was based on a Garden of Eden view of nature, in which plant communities are perceived as unchanging and what constitutes "native" is considered absolute and enduring. However, climate change is forcing conservationists not just to think outside the box but to recognize that the box itself has moved—and will continue to move for the foreseeable future. They are now scrambling to plan for future conditions, despite the fact that they don't fully understand how plants will behave when forced into areas where they currently do not exist, under conditions that are not yet precisely known. Peter Raven, director emeritus of Missouri Botanical Garden, points out that underlying traditional conservation practices "was always the notion that at some future date the plants would be reintroduced" to their native habitats and maintain themselves again. In an age of global warming, however, their native habitats are faced with change so fundamental that the plants may not be able to survive there, and it isn't clear where the plants can successfully be reintroduced.

As the climate changes, so will the definition of what is native and where. "We have a list of plants we consider native now," says Bill Brumback, conservation director at the New England Wild Flower Society, which has pioneered a regional approach to plant conservation. But with climate change, he says, what is considered native will be a moving target. What's more, there's little guidance for how natural areas should be managed when the development of novel species assemblages with no current counterparts is virtually inevitable. New conservation approaches are required to move us from the world we have known to one we have never seen.

Banking on Seed

Botanical gardens are increasingly seen as bridges to this future. Their efforts to conserve species in cultivation will continue to play a key role in safekeeping native plants until the climate has become stable enough to reestablish them in the wild. According to a survey by Botanic Gardens Conservation International, which represents over 700 members, mostly botanic gardens, in 118 countries, more than 100,000 of the world's plants are currently held in botanic gardens around the world, although these plant collections don't come anywhere near representing the genetic diversity of the species. More than 700 imperiled species in the U.S. are protected in the National Collection of Endangered Plants, coordinated by the Center for Plant Conservation, a network of the country's leading botanic gardens.

Botanic gardens are also collecting seeds for safekeeping in seed banks where, stored at very low temperatures, they can remain viable for a century or more and be used in future conservation efforts. The Millennium Seed Bank, an international project launched by the Royal Botanic Gardens, Kew, in 2000, has already collected seeds of 10 percent of the planet's wild plants and aims to save 25 percent by 2020.

Seeds of Success, a partnership of the federal Bureau of Land Management, the Millennium Seed Bank, and other groups, including a number of American botanic gardens, was established in 2001 to collect and conserve seeds of native U.S. plants.

Beyond securing an important reservoir of the planet's plant life, the broader outlines of a new conservation strategy are beginning to take shape. It's becoming apparent that conservationists must step up efforts to identify and protect species that may not be at risk now but are likely to be in the future. As part of its strategy for confronting climate change, NatureServe, a nationwide network of biological inventories known as natural heritage programs, has developed a vulnerability index to identify those species at greatest risk. At the top of the list are plants and animals whose habitat may disappear entirely. Rising temperatures are driving many alpine plants, for example, to higher elevations where it is cooler, but eventually they will reach the mountaintops and have no place to go. Plants with small ranges, like the Florida torreya, are also considered especially vulnerable, as are those whose survival depends on a so-called synchronous relationship with a pollinator or other species that may be responding to climate change at a different rate.

Some states have begun analyzing the vulnerability of the various habitats within their borders and evaluating their options for intervention. Massachusetts has found that spruce-fir forest, for example, is particularly at risk due to climate change. Knowing this, should conservationists make a concerted effort to preserve this habitat in the Bay State? Probably not, says the New England Wild Flower Society's Brumback. But it does make sense to collect and bank seeds from the plants in these at-risk habitats, he adds.

Rethinking Nature Preserves

Meanwhile, concepts of preserve design and management are changing to adjust to the new realities as they develop. Conservation biologists have explored the implications of reserve size, shape, and location for the conservation of biodiversity, but the science of designing a system of protected areas to accommodate climate change is still in its infancy.

There is a consensus that increasing the resilience of current preserves—their capacity to persist and absorb change—is crucial. In part, this involves continuing ongoing efforts to increase the number of individuals of local species and establish new populations: The more plants there are, the greater the chance that some will survive in suitable microsites or refugia in the face of climate change. In addition, more individual plants in a population generally results in increased genetic diversity and a higher likelihood that some members of the species will evolve and persist. Another strategy might be to introduce genotypes of the same species from warmer regions, which may be better adapted to the changing climate.

However, conservation efforts will fail if they focus solely on protecting areas that are home to native plants right now but won't be able to support them in the decades ahead. It's critical to identify the places that will be the climate-change refugia of the future. Computer models that relate species ranges to habitats and climates can help researchers predict where plants are likely to experience extreme turnover and which areas will probably continue to support a large portion of the species they currently contain. The latter areas should be high priorities for protection and restoration efforts. Because geological and topographic diversity is believed to be a major driver of species diversity, another approach gaining recognition stresses the necessity of protecting the range of landscape features, from limestone valley bottoms to serpentine soils and high-elevation granite slopes, that support plant diversity today and will likely continue to promote it as the climate changes, ranges shift, and new communities of species form.

The ability of species to survive in and traverse the larger landscape outside protected areas as their ranges shift is also critical. There's broad agreement that steps must be taken to identify and protect migration corridors—large, continuous, relatively undisturbed tracts of land most likely to enable plants and animals to successfully rearrange themselves. It may be necessary to forge agreements with landowners that include rights to future use of their land for conservation and encourage activities that result in the least ecological disturbance, such as no-till agriculture, sustainable forestry, and even low-density housing.

And if all this weren't complicated enough, conservation in the age of climate change must be done on a regional basis and across local, state, and international boundaries.

Assisted Migration

"We have to come up with names for these plants!" Connie Barlow declared as we trooped up the slope of the Corneille Bryan Native Garden in Lake Janaluska, North Carolina, carting ten little Florida torreyas. The potted seedlings were about to stir up one of the biggest controversies in contemporary conservation science. A petite and resolute woman in a tan-and-black dress, Keens, and a baseball cap, Barlow reeled off the names of a motley collection of botanists and conservation heroes: John Muir, Asa Gray, Aldo Leopold, Edward Abbey. "We need a lady here!" she proclaimed. Rachel Carson, Julia Butterfly Hill, and Wangari Matthai were added to the list.

Accompanying Barlow were other members of a loosely organized group who call themselves the Torreya Guardians, lugging buckets of lime and other soil amendments up the narrow ravine, where a spectacular assortment of Appalachian wildflowers were blooming on either side of a trickling stream. For the past few years these citizen activists had been laying the groundwork to move the storied tree to cooler latitudes to save it from climate change.

Growing seed taken surreptitiously from the wild and transplanting it on public lands would be illegal. However, the Torreya Guardians began distributing seeds donated by a public garden in North Carolina to individuals and institutions willing to commit to the perfectly legal proposition of germinating the seed and growing groves of the resulting seedlings in wild forests on private lands.

On that perfect summer day in late July, the small band of modern-day Noahs defied the rules of the conservation science establishment, moving 31 tiny trees obtained from one of the few commercial sources propagating and selling Florida torreya plants some 400 miles north of the species' current natural range to two sites in the North Carolina mountains. By introducing a species to a new environment, well outside its native habitat, they did precisely what conservation biologists have been urging people not to do at a time when invasive nonnative plants and animals pose one of the gravest threats to natural areas. Their action has intensified the debate over using "assisted migration" as a tool for saving species unable to keep pace with rapidly changing conditions on their own. It has also sparked a new controversy about how far citizen activists should go to help endangered species.

A few short years ago most scientists considered assisted migration, also called managed relocation, all but inconceivable. Now guidelines and best practices are being thrashed out in prestigious journals. University of Notre Dame biologist Jessica Hellmann, one of the leaders of a working group of biologists, ethicists, and legal scholars who published a decision-making framework for assisted migration in 2009, notes that it is a huge leap for her and her colleagues. "Many of us became biologists because we love wild places and want to preserve them," she says. "Traditionally, we have studied what the world *is* like. Moving things for climate change is a totally different ballgame. Now the question is what the world *should be* like and what we *want it to be* like. That feels like a big line we're crossing."

For Connie Barlow, moving the Florida torreya north is about restoring the species to its former home. Barlow is used to thinking in what she calls "deep time." Her book, *The Ghosts of Evolution*, paints a new picture of the ecological catastrophe that occurred at the end of the last ice age when North America's mammoths and other animals went extinct and left some native plants without their natural seed dispersers. She speculates that the Florida torreya may be one of these plants.

But with conditions changing at such a rapid clip, scientists will be doing their own assisted migrations before too long. Currently, there is no officially sanctioned plan to relocate the Florida torreya. However, Kay Havens and her colleagues at the Chicago Botanic Garden are beginning to test the feasibility of assisted migration for the dune thistle (*Cirsium pitcheri*), a federally threatened wildflower with woolly white leaves and puffy cream or pink summer blossoms that has been driven by development and drought from much of its habitat along the western Great Lakes. Climate change is likely to make its current habitats even warmer and drier.

Novel Plant Communities

As alpine meadows and maple forests morph into new ecological entities, a growing number of scientists are recognizing that conservation measures even more radical than assisted migration of individual species may be necessary. Historically authentic plant communities such as tall-grass prairie, they point out, are increasingly rare. In fact, most have been so altered by changing conditions and nonnative species that they may already qualify as novel ecosystems. It may be essential to manage the ongoing development of these newfangled communities—or even *create* them—to protect species and important ecological processes.

The small group of Torreya Guardians continued on from Lake Janaluska to private land in nearby Waynesville, the next stop on the Florida torreya's extraordinary journey. There, on a little bluff at about 3,800 feet elevation, down a trail and across a ravine, 21 seedlings were nestled among sourwood, striped maple, and sassafras, amid struggling stump sprouts of once towering American chestnut trees ravaged by blight and hemlocks succumbing to the hemlock woolly adelgid, a fuzzy, aphidlike insect from Asia that is the latest scourge of the eastern forests.

As climate change intensifies, humans inevitably will be the movers of last resort for a growing number of plants and animals. In fact, the transformation of almost biblical proportions we have unleashed on the land will be so staggeringly complicated and costly that public funds and scientific manpower will likely be stretched to the limits just managing species that play major ecological roles. There's already speculation that the fate of so-called non-keystone species may be left to citizen groups like the Torreya Guardians.

While scientists weigh the wisdom of once unimaginable measures such as assisted migration, there is poetic justice in the fact that the Florida torreya, thought by some to be the gopher wood of Noah's ark, has come to symbolize our struggle to do right by this jumbled new world we have created. Boston University's Richard Primack concedes that assisted migration of imperiled plants risks unleashing invasive species. But, he says, there is a much more serious danger: "that our efforts to move them will fail."

Designing a Restoration Garden

Judith Larner Lowry

The weeks before our annual open house fluctuate between busy and frantic. I race back and forth, wanting our one-acre backyard restoration garden to be as gorgeous as possible, replete with many of the showy and also the less showy species that might at one time have grown here. At the same time, I want it to reflect the guidelines for habitat restoration gardening that have evolved here through the years.

As I patrol the grounds to enforce our zero tolerance policy for weeds, aimed today at Bermuda buttercup (*Oxalis pes-caprae*), I reflect on the long journey that has brought me to this day. It began with coyote bush....

A large idea had begun sizzling within me almost as soon as I moved with my family to Bolinas, a town on the northern coast of California surrounded by state and national parks. Simply put, I believed that my garden could draw upon a palette of locally native flora, and in that way support the locally native fauna as well as satisfy my yearning to be surrounded by the plants native to my new home territory.

Walks into the surrounding protected land revealed to me that these lands were actually not all that well protected. I realized that some of my neighbors' gardens were part of the problem, acting as sources for invasive plant species threatening the integrity of our public lands. I began to tentatively express a plan to restore local flora, beginning with our gardens.

It was an idea in general not well received at the time, in the early 1980s. Some of my new neighbors felt that their gardening choices were being disparaged by an arrogant newcomer. I spent the next 30 years honing my arguments, building my business, and learning how to be tactful. Since then, the number of native plant gardens in Bolinas has grown from 0 to about 90, and my own yard has become a demonstration garden and vibrant seed nursery supporting homeowner habitat restoration projects.

Choosing a Keynote Plant Species

I became even more unpopular through championing coyote bush (*Baccharis pilularis*), a native shrub thought by some to be undistinguished and not "garden worthy" and by others to be too aggressive. It became my garden "totem," or keynote plant, as I searched for clues to what had historically grown on the site of my garden and its environs. Where

The author adopted coyote bush (*Baccharis pilularis*) as the keynote plant for a restoration garden that showcases the plants native to northern coastal California.

I found intact hillsides of close-hugging coastal scrub and chaparral species, a rugged gray and green mantle preventing erosion, coyote bush was the foundation.

A small island of coyote bush was the only remaining native habitat in my one-acre garden. Rustling with bird and insect life every time I walked by, it caused me to look more closely. Though not found on the lists of California's showiest native shrubs, coyote bush is a generous host, adept at playing many roles to keep the party going. In the fall, when not much else is blooming, it is covered with fluffy white blossoms, a draw for West Coast lady butterflies, tachina flies, and more than 200 other invertebrates. It also provides habitat for brush rabbits, mountain beaver, garter snakes, and a host of other fauna.

In some situations, it makes a hospitable nursery for oak (*Quercus*) seedlings, California hazelnut seedlings (*Corylus cornuta* var. *californica*), and other woodland components sown by jays and squirrels. In time, a patch of coyote bush may give way to an oak forest or hazel copse. Elsewhere, at cliff edge or coastal bluff, it is a climax species, last in the line of natural succession. Its tenacious roots penetrate the unstable cliffs both widely and deeply. Coyote bush can handle high winds and salt spray while remaining green and shapely.

My hiking investigations revealed that the native herbaceous species that grow with coyote bush were frequently being displaced by Himalayan blackberry (*Rubus armeniacus*), weedy grasses, and other rampant invaders like cape ivy (*Delairea odorata*), English ivy (*Hedera helix*), common teasel (*Dipsacus fullonum*), and fennel (*Foeniculum vulgare*). My first horticultural act was to remove those invaders from my own coyote bush island. My second was to start planting coyote bush throughout the garden. I used both the shrub form, *Baccharis pilularis* subsp. *consanguinea*, and the dwarf, groundcover form, *B. pilularis* subsp. *pilularis*.

The generous use of coyote bush gave the garden a visual flow throughout the year. Adding other evergreen shrubs, like California sagebrush (*Artemisia californica*), coffeeberry (*Rhamnus californica*), and blueblossom (*Ceanothus thyrsiflorus*), enriched the visual mosaic, the flowering insect draw, and the fruit supply for birds. Shrub groupings surrounding open areas made the garden seem larger, divided it into distinctive rooms, and provided many local creatures with what they wanted. Today, a weeding day, I am doubly grateful for these shrubby areas, where little weeding is required.

Piggyback Conservation in the Backyard

One way I thought about my garden design in the early days was in terms of the requirements of the California valley quail, a species historically inhabiting my area. As a favored game bird with declining populations, the quail's plant preferences have been much studied and make an appealing template for the restoration garden. (In this, it may resemble the northern bobwhite of the eastern U.S., another game bird whose population has seriously declined but whose numbers also respond well to habitat restoration.) Quail also have the invaluable ability to share their domestic lives with close-by humans, parading their young across our yards and charming us into the desire to do whatever we can to further their prospects.

I provided our quail open areas with bunchgrasses, lupines, composites like goldfields (*Lasthenia glabrata*), and redmaids (*Calandrinia ciliata*)—all favored quail food. Surrounding these "dining rooms" are sheltered areas for hanging out comprised of coyote bush and the other shrubs listed above. Fast-growing coast live oaks (*Quercus agrifolia*) serve as roosting perches. Nesting habitat is provided by large bunchgrasses such as California fescue (*Festuca californica*), Pacific reedgrass (*Calamagrostis nutkaensis*) and, again, coyote bush.

Our quail like the design plan, as do wrentits, bushtits, rufus-sided towhees, robins, and scores of other birds, butterflies, beetles, and bees. In ecological restoration, this is called "piggyback conservation," wherein efforts to preserve the more charismatic fauna, like the handsome, noisy quail, also benefit the less well-known animals.

My garden has taught me that designing for wildlife is also designing for humans. Our eyes and our deep wiring seem attuned to the same spatial configurations that the creatures like. Good garden design is frequently good restoration practice, resulting in a sense of peace, enclosure, and ineffable "rightness" often remarked upon by visitors.

Rebuilding a Local Plant Community

Through coyote bush, I found myself drawn into the ecology of the whole plant association called "northern coastal scrub," including California sagebrush, sticky monkeyflower (*Mimulus aurantiacus*), western sword fern (*Polystichum munitum*), and a host of forbs (broad-leafed herbs).

It became my goal to bring those plants into my one-acre garden and deepen my relationship with them beyond that of a nodding acquaintance. While leading tours of my garden, I saw myself repeatedly pointing to easy-to-love native forbs like peppermint candy flower (*Claytonia sibirica*), seaside bird's-foot trefoil (*Lotus formosissimus*), or Point Reyes checkerbloom (*Sidalcea calycosa* subsp. *rhizomata*). I would then recall where I originally saw that wildflower in the so-called protected land around our town, ending with the news that the original area has since been taken over by vinca, French broom, or fennel.

Given a chance, all of these plants were vigorous, hardy, drought tolerant, and made a strong and splendid contribution to the insect and bird life of the garden. Some were essential to the survival of certain insects; others drew hummingbirds, butterflies, and birds. Because of their low stature, they could not withstand the incursions of taller weedy species. Adding them to the garden became a focus—an ongoing project that we call "fostering forbs."

Design Guidelines for Restoration Gardening

Use nearby native plant communities as models. Look for site conditions similar to those of your garden for the plant palette and vegetation architecture.

Choose a keynote native shrub or tree species to provide the bones of your design and habitat resources. Repetition throughout the garden—of a single species or of a grouping—leads to harmony. Variation with other plants lends interest and habitat for a diverse array of wildlife.

Choose a keynote native bird, possibly nonmigratory, to inspire your plant choices and garden structure. The conditions it prefers will draw other local fauna too.

Grow plants with native insects in mind. Organizations that support insects, such as the Xerxes Society, the North American Butterfly Society, and Pollinator Partnerships, supply information on local plant-insect relationships.

Invite beneficial native bees into your garden. First, eliminate toxic chemicals. Then, plant native plants. Finally, supply bare dirt as well as dead twigs for native bee nurseries.

Be mindful of your region's seasonality and don't seek to circumvent it with horticultural overrides. In California, this might be called learning to love brown. In the colder climes, learn to love winter, with its responses both subtle and dramatic to lowered temperatures. Avoid usually fruitless attempts to plant species not locally hardy, and use that energy instead to experiment with local natives perhaps not often seen in the garden.

Employ a range of maintenance strategies, including indigenous plant management techniques like harvesting and pruning to mimic natural fire regimes. Another approach involves spending more grooming time on areas around the house (or perhaps near the street) and letting the hedges or designated wilder areas do their thing unimpeded (such as leaving flower stalks for winter birds).

Foster forbs. Give special attention to the most threatened ones, the annual and perennial wildflowers whose size makes them most vulnerable to weed invasions.

Though restoration gardening has serious goals, remember that horticultural play is still allowed. Train an oak sapling into the shape of a trellis. Use attractive containers to set off the qualities of forbs that would otherwise go unnoticed. Bring in garden art that expresses your love of place. Have fun!

We began with Douglas meadowfoam (*Limnanthes douglasii*), one of several meadowfoam species native to California. I first collected this beautiful low-growing annual wildflower in a nearby hayfield and found it to be astonishingly persistent in the garden, returning and spreading year after year. I decided to dedicate a significant area to what we called the meadowfoam lawn.

After several months of lush growth in late fall and early winter, the meadowfoam blooms for two to three months in early spring. From a distance, the yellow and white petals are a buttery, luscious blur. The sight is so gorgeous that when the stress of open house preparation becomes too great, my employees and I ask each other, "Have you had your meadowfoam moment today?" A trip to the meadow includes time to tune into the diverse bee life it fosters.

After the flowers fade and the plants go to seed and die—a seven-month process— the area is kept free of vegetation for the next five months, till the rains come again in the fall. To make the area acceptable to the gardener's eye, I group several wooden lawn chairs in the middle.

The Virtues of Bare Dirt

A bare dirt area is a sacrifice that would be harder to make in a smaller garden, and it is still challenging for a gardener seeking to proselytize native plants. It is a goal of our open house to explain this uncommon garden feature and the ecological perspective it represents.

The meadowfoam lawn honors the vernal ponds—seasonal wetlands that used to be everywhere in my town—and the unique vegetation that grew around them, which includes meadowfoam. We model an acceptance of the seasonality of California's annual wildflowers, including baby blue eyes (*Nemophila menziesii*), tidy tips (*Layia platyglossa*), goldfields, globe gilia (*Gilia capitata*), lupines (*Lupinus* species), and many more, which germinate with the fall and winter rains, come into bloom with the spring sun, and go to seed and die in the summer. This scenario creates the great California pageant of annual spring-blooming wildflowers.

I didn't understand at first that I was also honoring the California phenomenon of seasonally bare dirt. When native wildflowers die or native perennials go dormant, nonnative weeds can move into the resulting bare soil and outcompete them before they can return from seed or dormancy. The continued movement into California of plants from elsewhere has in many places eliminated seasonal bare dirt.

Nor did I understand other benefits that seasonal dirt patch would confer. Oval indentations in the brown dirt indicate that the quail like to dust-bathe here. From a distance, tiny dust clouds appear on good bathing days from our quail spa.

Habitat for Invertebrates

No matter where you live in the U.S., bare dirt is important for fostering native bees: About two thirds of North America's bees are ground-nesting species—solitary animals that build chambers in the ground, where they lay single eggs and provision them with pollen and nectar "loaves." My restoration garden is an effort to provide a haven for some of California's 1,600 bee species, many of which need bare dirt.

When trying to restore insect habitat, the plot invariably thickens. We all know that many flowers, both native and nonnative, attract bees and other insects, but what is not well known is that in the case of some insects, only the flowers they coevolved with give them the nectar and/or pollen they need to survive. In other cases, only the insects the flowers coevolved with provide those plants with the means for optimum reproduction.

The seed ripening of meadowfoam tells a unique coevolutionary story. When a solitary native bee called *Andrena limnanthis* is present for pollination, each flower can produce five smooth round seeds the size of lentils. Without that bee, pollination is usually partial, producing only two or three frequently smaller seeds. *Andrena limnanthis* is an oligolege, or specialist pollinator, that visits only meadowfoam species. When a long drought caused a meadowfoam failure in our garden, this bee waited four years for the plant to return before emerging from its underground nest.

Researchers have found that native plants are significantly better at fostering native pollinators than nonnative plants. Looking beyond nectar and pollen resources, some butterflies, such as monarchs, need the chemical substances toxic to their predators that are obtained only from certain host plants, such as milkweed. The extinction or diminishment of certain native plant populations has led to the disappearance of a significant number of host-dependent butterflies. An example in my area is the mission blue butterfly, whose near extinction parallels the eclipse of its host plant the silver lupine (*Lupinus albifrons*) and other lupine species.

Do Try This at Home

Gardeners can ease the plight of their specialist insect friends by growing the plants with which these animals coevolved. It can be done in a way that provides both good habitat for wildlife and a pleasing visual display for people to enjoy. When designing for bees, create large patches of individual species of flowering plants, since bees forage most efficiently when they can remain in the behavior pattern associated with a certain kind of nectar and pollen extraction. Planting this way also increases the likelihood that pollen extracted from one species won't be wasted on another species.

In order to maximize the diversity of bees and other insects your garden can support, include flowers with simple, open forms, like asters, and those with more complex tubular forms, such as lupines and salvias. Provide a continuous sequence of bloom throughout the season so that the bees have a constant food source.

By planting even small patches of native plants, gardeners can support wildlife in rural and urban areas alike. City gardeners may not be able to help large fauna, but they can do a great deal for insect and bird species that can traverse fragmented urban landscapes. For instance, one dedicated group of gardeners in San Francisco is working to connect two populations of the endangered coastal green hairstreak butterfly by planting its host plants along the sidewalks that separate them.

The kind of habitat restoration work that can be done will vary from region to region. Gardeners in the Northeast may choose to restore woodland species lost from urban areas. Rural dwellers can make a positive impact by maintaining open, sunny, grassy areas on their land. Because of the decline of farming and the consequent regrowth of forests in the Northeast over the last century, species that thrive in open areas, such as the bronze copper, regal fritillary, and arogos skipper butterflies, are in trouble. New England cottontail rabbits and a whole suite of grassland birds are also of concern.

Schooled by the Garden

If the vocation of being human is to learn, my backyard restoration garden is a handy textbook, and also a notebook—a scrawling, messy, dirt- and water-stained record of how a garden based on local flora might evolve.

The knowledge my garden gives me is a greater in-depth understanding of the landscape in my vicinity, the "protected" land of county, state, and federal domain. There are few places where I can see as many native species (and as few nonnatives) as in my own garden. From this experience, I know with what fervor those few remaining wild places must be protected, and how fragile their status is.

I am often surprised to note that some dedicated conservationists and preservationists have home gardens that do not reflect their commitment to the natural world, which includes plants. They are used to thinking on a large scale, which we need. We also need the attention to detail, the unstinting dedication, and the hands-on effort that gardeners so generously offer.

These days, people frequently ask me the name of the handsome, rich green, perfectly round shrub that makes such an elegant foil for the other plants in our garden. I say, "Why, that's coyote bush." That's coyote bush when given space to grow, pruning when needed, and respect.

I don't know what your "coyote bush" will be, which locally native totem plant might thread its way through your garden with such grace and giving. Ideas from local floras and botanic gardens are invaluable resources, as are walks to nearby wild areas, preferably with knowledgeable guides. Through using local plant communities as models, some predictions can be made. But you cannot know in exactly which ways your site, small or large, with its particular location, history, and microclimate, will again become part of the story told by the plants and animals native to it, a story interrupted not all that long ago.

Nor can you predict what waking up to the guard quail's call on a summer morning will feel like, or how finding the chrysalis of a pipevine swallowtail on the large-leafed California pipevine draping over your fence will make your day. Now that I've experienced for 30 years this kind of surprise and gratitude on a daily basis, I can say with certainty: When you garden with the goal of returning to the land that which has been taken away, the gift keeps moving—in the gardener's direction.

Welcoming Wildlife into the Garden

Douglas W. Tallamy

Last summer my wife and I were privileged—but not accidental—participants in one of nature's special performances. A pair of birds nested in our yard. I know that doesn't sound very special. But when you think about what it took for that avian couple to successfully reproduce in our suburban setting, it becomes very special indeed.

I still remember the first time I saw the male blue grosbeak. I thought it was one of our many indigo buntings but soon realized it was a larger bird, had a beautiful streak of red on its wings, and produced a different song. At first, he spent all day singing. He would flex his azure crest, scan the ground from his perch on one of our ironwood trees, and sing his heart out. His goal was not to entertain me but to stake his claim to a breeding territory. He chose our property to raise his young because it's dotted with the small trees and shrubs that are perfect for concealing his nest. Even more important, the insects he needed to feed his nestlings are plentiful here.

It didn't take him long to find romance; a chocolate-colored female, lured by his melodies, found him and the quality of the territory he was guarding to her liking. Soon she started to construct a nest deep within an alternate-leaf dogwood tree. Blue grosbeaks are among the few birds that use molted snake skins as nesting material. The task of locating a suitable skin typically falls to the male, and at our house he was in luck: A black rat snake had left a four-foot skin near a groundhog hole in our meadow. Soon the grosbeak and his mate had woven the skin among grass blades and sticks to form what would become home for three nestlings. This was his only successful bout of reproduction that year, but he sang in celebration every morning at seven sharp until mid-September, when he and his mate departed for their overwintering grounds in southern Mexico.

Rebuilding Food Webs

Please remember that what I have described did not take place in a national park, or even in a small county preserve. It happened in our yard. It happened in our yard because we have built our landscape with all the bits of nature that blue grosbeaks require to make more blue grosbeaks. Once mown for hay, our property—a ten-acre

A complex native plant landscape welcomes wildlife by offering sheltered nesting spaces and fostering a local food web that provides resources throughout the seasons.

lot on the site of a former farm near Oxford, Pennsylvania—is now planted with young oaks, American elms, chestnuts, beeches, birches, eastern red cedars, black cherries, red maples, and plums. We have gray dogwoods, flowering dogwoods, and alternate-leaf dogwoods. There are also fringetrees and silverbells, as well as winterberries, inkberries, and viburnums. We have planted our yard with a diversity of plants that provide the food necessary for grosbeak reproduction. Our woody natives alone support well over a thousand species of caterpillars, as well as myriad other insects that are essential foods for young grosbeaks. After the fledglings leave the nest, these same plants supply the grosbeak family with seeds and berries to supplement their continued diet of insects.

We have the snake skins our grosbeaks use to build their nest because we have black rat snakes, black racers, milk snakes, ribbon snakes, ring-necked snakes, painted water snakes, and garter snakes on our property. We have these harmless reptiles because we have the mice, voles, shrews, salamanders, pollywogs, frogs, and toads that they eat, and because we have groundhog dens that are perfect places for snakes to avoid the weather extremes of winter and summer. And we have snake food because we have the plants that supply the insects and seeds eaten by mice, voles, shrews, and toads, and because we leave refuges of untrimmed grass for them so they can avoid being decapitated during Saturday mowings.

We have blue grosbeaks in our yard, as well as chipping sparrows, field sparrows, song sparrows, yellowthroats, willow flycatchers, chickadees, cedar waxwings, robins, cardinals, mockingbirds, bluebirds, brown thrashers, titmice, woodpeckers, wrens, and 40 other species of breeding birds because we have redundancy in each of their ecological requirements. If a mockingbird has already built a nest in a suitable dogwood, our grosbeaks can find an unoccupied dogwood—because we have many. If our black cherry trees don't support enough larvae of the promethea moth, white furcula, and small-eyed sphinx to satiate the baby grosbeaks, our oak trees will fill the void with unicorn caterpillars, red-humped oak worms, confused woodgrains, variable oak leaf caterpillars, and white-dotted prominents. If our black rat snakes shed their skins within a mole tunnel where the grosbeaks can't find them, our black racers will leave their sheds in plain view on one of our mown paths.

In short, we have built a landscape that guarantees a steady supply of all the resources needed by blue grosbeaks to successfully reproduce, a landscape with enough complexity to promote long-term balance and stability in the food webs it creates. We have lawn, but only in the areas we typically walk. At our house, grass carpet is not the default landscape, something we do with the land when we don't know what else to do. Rather, it is a mechanism for formalizing plant communities and for guiding us through our dense plantings.

Our gardens are not destroyed by sharing them with insects, as many people fear, because by encouraging populations of native insects, we are providing the food for the many animals that eat insects: the minute parasitic wasps that reproduce within stink bug and caterpillar eggs, the larger wasps that develop within the bodies of caterpillars and beetles; the assassin bugs and ambush bugs that help control our fall web worms and treehoppers; the damsel bugs that eat plant bug and lace bug eggs; the jumping spiders that pounce on unsuspecting leafhoppers; the entomopathogenic fungi that turn flies and ants into monuments of spores; and the viruses that turn caterpillars into mush. We also have big-headed flies that make sure we don't have too many planthoppers; small-headed flies that make sure we don't have too many spiders; thick-headed flies that make sure we don't have too many paper wasps; and long-legged flies that make sure we don't have too many aphids. But our garden ecosystem would not remain balanced without help from local vertebrates: the frogs and toads and salamanders and foxes and possums and raccoons and white-footed mice—and above all, the *birds*, which eat insects from morning till dusk.

An Informal Experiment

We bought our property 11 years ago, one of a number of 10-acre lots resulting from the subdivision of a 150-acre farm. Our immediate neighbors also purchased a single, 10-acre lot. Both households had the usual choices about how to manage their property. My wife and I (an entomologist by trade) wanted to manage for biodiversity: to do our best to restore the patchwork of forest, meadows, and wetlands that once characterized southeastern Pennsylvania. Our motivation was simple and just a little bit selfish: We enjoy nature and hoped to landscape in a way that brought us into daily contact with its many rewards.

Our neighbors chose the more traditional approach to land management, landscaping their property for neatness, aesthetics, and conformity. The current custom dictates that a property, regardless of its size or location, be planted in lawn that is meticulously maintained and sparsely decorated with standard ornamental plants from Asia and Europe. Throughout the U.S., adherence to this social norm is a measure of stewardship, character, industry, wealth, and status. Our neighbors tolerate our differences in land management because they are nice people and because they have erected an effective screen of Douglas firs that block their view of our less-groomed property.

Unbeknownst to any of us at the time, we had inadvertently embarked on a long-term experiment measuring the supply of ecosystem services from different models of suburban landscaping. Ten years into this experiment, all sorts of interesting comparisons can now be made: We could measure with confidence how well each of our yards sequesters carbon, filters pollutants from rainwater before it leaves our properties, holds rainwater on-site for maximum water table recharge, and sustains viable populations of plants and animals. We could compare the carbon footprint associated with maintaining each landscape and the number of bird species that have found our yards acceptable breeding sites. We could also compare the number of migratory birds that stop to rest and refuel as they race north to breed in the spring and retreat south to overwintering grounds in the fall.

We could find answers to such questions as, Which property will enable our kids and their kids to catch more lightning bugs on June evenings, marvel over the life cycle of the cecropia or polyphemus moth, and watch pollywogs grow little legs and lose their tails? Which of our homes is cooled by summer shade trees or has lower heating bills because of strategically placed windbreaks of vegetation? Which property remains green during summer droughts with no artificial irrigation? Which property provides more pollination services by nurturing larger and more diverse populations of native bees?

Diversity Matters

I have only begun to tabulate the results, but so far the differences are striking. We now have 103 species of native woody plants on our property, while our neighbors have 4; of the 16 species of ornamental plants that adorn their yard, 13 are from Asia. Five of their favorite landscape plants—Callery pear (*Pyrus calleryana*), burning bush (*Euonymus elatus*), Japanese honeysuckle (*Lonicera japonica*), princess tree (*Paulownia tomentosa*), and Chinese silvergrass (*Miscanthus sinensis*)—are highly invasive and pop up uninvited on our property every year. Our neighbors' property invariably looks neat and attractive; we enjoy a less controlled profusion of native herbaceous annuals and perennials, including several goldenrods, asters, warm-season grasses, spring ephemerals, rudbeckias, sunflowers, blackberries, wild strawberries, milkweeds, dogbanes, phloxes, violets, and eupatoriums. We have allocated 5 percent of our property to lawn, mostly in the form of mown paths, while 71 percent of our neighbor's 10 acres is in weed-free lawn that is manicured to an even 1½ inches in height, twice a week.

We have planted 12 species of oak in our yard for three reasons: We like oaks; oaks produce the greatest number of caterpillar species (bird food) of any plant in the mid-Atlantic states; and oaks sequester the most carbon of any regional hardwood. Our neighbors have no oaks on their property. And so it goes. I offer such statistics not to be judgmental but to raise awareness about the unavoidable consequences of traditional landscaping practices, consequences about which most homeowners have not been informed when making choices about their gardens.

Landscape plants are more than decorations! Used properly, they clean and store water, filter air pollutants, reduce heating and cooling bills, sequester carbon dioxide, prevent floods, and maintain food webs; that is, they deliver ecosystem services that are essential to human well-being. The natural areas that once supplied such services for us are now so small and isolated that we need to rebuild functioning ecosystems in our yards...everywhere. And we can do this only with plants. Every time we add an additional human to the earth, we need more plants, not fewer, in our landscapes.

Traditional, lawn-dominated landscapes are biologically barren areas that harbor few species, support few natural processes, and thus create few ecosystem services. We can no longer afford landscapes that don't include life support systems, not if we want to be alive ourselves in the future.

If You Plant Natives, Wildlife Will Come

My wife and I garden with a heavy bias toward plants that have been part of local food webs for millennia because that's the only way the nature we love will be able to thrive in our yard. Ten years ago, our property was overrun with invasive plants from Asia. We realized that to see local animals, we would have to keep the animals local; and to keep animals local, we would have to restore the food webs that sustain them. Hence our use of native plants, which provide the best—and in most cases, the only—food resources for our native wildlife, particularly insects, the protein source for so many of our favorite animals.

Are there nonnative plants that provide food for native insects? Certainly, particularly ones that offer nectar for butterflies and bees. But there are no cases where plants that evolved elsewhere support insect communities that are more diverse and more abundant than those supported by native plant communities. The Asian butterfly bush (*Buddleja davidii*) that attracts so many butterflies to your yard does not serve as a larval host plant for any eastern butterflies. If, in our zeal to attract butterflies to our gardens, we only planted alien nectar plants like butterfly bush, we would be left with no butterflies at all, because their native larval hosts—plants such as black cherry, willows, hackberry, and oaks—would be eliminated from managed landscapes.

The Callery pears that line the streets in my neighborhood support one species of caterpillar; were the streets lined with native oaks trees, 534 species of caterpillar could be available for hungry birds. Or imagine a neighborhood in which deodor cedars from the Himalayas (a popular ornamental tree on the West Coast) were replaced with native pines. Our native pine white butterfly is able to develop on deodar cedars, but if we substituted pines for cedars, over 200 other species of moths and butterflies that can only eat native pines would regain their host plants. I could go on.

My wife and I have been enormously enriched by our restoration. Rather than ducking inside to avoid the roar of a lawn mower, the nasally whine of a leaf blower, or the sputtering of a weed whacker, we can now set our watches by the daily sounds of the animals that call our yard home: the midnight scream of our mother fox as she delineates the territory in which she is raising her seven kits; the dawn chorus of our resident and migrant birds; the midmorning buzz of our annual cicadas as they call for mates; the afternoon whistle of our sentry groundhog as she warns her relatives that a red-tailed hawk is nearby; the late-afternoon hum of our ruby-throated hummingbird as he hovers in front of the coral honeysuckle flowers; the crepuscular echoes of our spring peepers and toads in the marsh; and of course, the 7 a.m. melody of our blue grosbeak male.

Adventures in Native Plant Propagation

William Cullina

Plant propagation—the phrase has an intimidating, scientific detachment about it that suggests stainless steel tabletops and researchers in white lab coats performing unnatural manipulations on unsuspecting plants. I think many would-be propagators are scared off by the mere term! At its root, though, plant propagation is just the simple art of making more, multiplying—spreading the love, as I like to say. Though I have propagated what must be approaching a million plants in my lifetime, I find it just as thrilling now as I always have to take one crested iris and divide it into 20 or collect a Baggie full of fluff from a blazing star in the fall and by spring be looking at 400 small seedlings poking up through the earth.

I began gardening at about the age of five by helping my mother plant the vegetable patch and redistribute wildflowers in our yard; but my first official act of propagation came when I was in the fourth grade and had the opportunity to enroll in weekend classes at a science center nearby. In between astronomy and physics, we learned how to root stem sections of a Christmas cactus in sand. I can still remember the excitement I felt when we pulled out the stems a few weeks later to reveal a startling shag of roots emerging from the lower joints. I was hooked.

I had that Christmas cactus all through high school and even took a piece of it to college. Sadly, the original plant grew so large that one year my mother "forgot" to bring it in before first frost, and later, I also lost its offspring during one of my many moves. Therefore, you can imagine my surprise and delight when I ran into my college roommate's girlfriend a few years ago, and she told me she still had a plant rooted from a stem that I had given her! Just three weeks prior to writing this essay, she sent me a padded envelope stuffed with a dozen pieces that are now rooting in the greenhouse at work. After 35 years, I am again rooting cuttings of this selfsame *Schlumbergera* × *buckleyi*.

My recent reunion with the prodigal cactus illustrates five essential things about plant propagation: It's easy, inexpensive, and infectious, and it fosters connections with plants—and friendships with fellow plant lovers—like nothing else in horticulture can.

The City of New York Greenbelt Native Plant Center propagates species like eastern marsh fern (*Thelypteris palustris*), which is designated "vulnerable" in New York State.

Cultivating Patience

Plant propagation can be easy, but it is not often instantaneous. It is very similar to cooking from scratch—if you have some basic equipment and follow the recipes, you'll be successful. Not everyone can be a professional plant propagator (or a celebrity chef, for that matter), but somewhere in between blowing on dandelion fluff and setting up a basement tissue-culture lab, you'll find a happy medium where you can be nicely supplied with plants.

I imagine that almost every gardener has cleaved a perennial in two with a shovel once or twice. Division is the simplest and most immediate form of propagation, and many herbaceous species (along with some woody ones) can be multiplied this way. In nurseries, division is the preferred method for many of the slower-growing woodland wildflowers, and it is remarkable how fast you can go from a single plant to 20. Propagating native plants from seed is a bit more challenging, especially if your experience is limited to raising annuals like tomatoes and marigolds. Still, raising seedlings requires very little equipment and can be achieved if you have some patience.

For woodland wildflowers like trilliums (*Trillium* species), twinleaf (*Jeffersonia diphylla*), Solomon's seal (*Polygonatum* species), and the like, your patience will surely be tried. Most natives (at least in the Northeast) need a period of damp, winter chill to germinate. These plants often take two years to sprout and two more to grow to a size presentable enough for the garden or friends. When I mention this fact to students, I always hear a few muffled groans. It can seem daunting to get started with some of these slow-growing, yet coveted, species. However, get started you must, and within a year or two you will have enough seedlings to keep you busy while the younger ones mature. I once worked for a distinguished plant breeder who was still making *Rhododendron* hybrids into his 80s. "Waiting another ten years for these to mature gives me something to live for," he would say with a smile. The good news is that many wildflowers and a good number of shrubs will germinate after only a few weeks or months and may even bloom the first season.

The Benefits of Doing It Yourself

The thing you will notice once propagation fever takes hold is how quickly your garden fills up and how slowly your garden budget drains down. Countless times I've bought a small, albeit pricey, pot of some treasured rarity and within a few years had a dozen more. Collecting and germinating your own seeds costs even less and allows you access to many species unavailable commercially.

This last point is especially important when it comes to native plants. Even with the plethora of native plant nurseries that have sprung up over the past 20 years, many wonderful species are still practically unavailable in the trade. Just yesterday I admired a lovely hobblebush viburnum (*Viburnum lantanoides*, syn. *V. alnifolium*) blooming in the woods next to our local school on Southport Island, Maine, yet try to find this plant for sale anywhere.

Lack of availability was the impetus behind the creation of the native plant nursery at the New England Wild Flower Society (NEWFS), which I ran for 13 years. Before coming to NEWFS, I worked for several years at Niche Gardens, in North Carolina. Though I have always been a naturalist and gardener at heart, it was at Niche that my interest in natives and passion for propagation came together in a big way. Learning that I could make a real difference by growing and popularizing our native wildflowers, shrubs, and trees was truly empowering and highly infectious.

The knowledge that I gained working for these two organizations is immeasurable. I even learned how to cut down on the propagation time of some of the trickier native plants. For example, the seeds of the hobblebush ripen in late summer, and we found that if we collected them as the fruits began to blush and then cleaned off the flesh, seeds would sprout a root before frost and send up a set of fat cotyledons the following spring. Prior to this discovery, we used to wait until the berries were mature before collecting the seed, and this delay added a year to the germination time. Hobblebush is a slow-growing species, but after two years of gentle coaxing, we could produce saleable seedlings.

Working with the hobblebush also taught me a very valuable lesson about plant genetics and microevolution. One year, we collected seeds near where I live along mid-coast Maine, as well as near my former house in northeastern Connecticut. The following spring, we had a tremendous crop of seedlings growing lustily in the greenhouse in western Massachusetts. But that summer was a hot one, and by its end, the Maine plants had withered and died, whereas their Connecticut cousins were doing well. Though separated by only 150 miles, the parent populations of these plants had slowly adapted over many centuries to the idiosyncrasies of their own particular climate. The Maine plants would doubtless have thrived here on cool, foggy Southport Island; the Connecticut plants survived precisely because they were better adapted to a warmer climate father south. Though the two sets of plants belonged to the same species, they were genetically different—or more technically, had different "genotypes"—having evolved over time in response to different local conditions.

Collecting Seeds

Provenance (where individual plants originate) has importance for scientists studying gene flow and evolution; it also has practical importance for gardeners, landscapers, and restoration practitioners as we try to grow the plants best suited to our particular place. While nurseries are now paying more attention to provenance and the underlying concept of different genotypes when they source material, for all intents and purposes, the only sure way to acquire truly local—and locally adapted—plants is to collect seed or cuttings from your own woods, roadsides, and meadows and grow them yourself.

Seed collection is an art in and of itself, but here are a few tips to get you started. I try to collect seeds from wild plants when possible, so I know their locality and can avoid problems with chance hybridization, which often occurs among related species in gardens. Avoid rare species, and ask permission of landowners before harvesting from their property. Collecting on public land requires special permission, so check first with local authorities about what permits are needed. It's better to take a few seeds from a number of plants rather than a lot from just a few. There is no set time that seeds mature, but start looking for them four to eight weeks after flowering. With few exceptions, seeds are mature when the seed coat has turned from white or green to some shade of tan or brown. If the seeds grow inside a fleshy fruit, wait until you see the fruits begin to ripen; if they form inside a pod or capsule, they are mature when the vessel turns brown and starts to dry.

Though the seeds of most species can be air-dried, cleaned, and then stored in a paper envelope until fall seed-sowing time comes around, those of some species—especially woodland wildflowers and nut-bearing trees—should be planted as soon as they are harvested and cleaned. A kitchen sieve, old rolling pin, and a few manila envelopes will make separating seed from chaff and pods less of a chore. The easiest way to germinate seeds is to sow them in pots in summer or fall (the timing depends on the species) and place these in an outdoor cold frame until they germinate. A simple wooden frame sunk partway in the ground and covered with burlap sacks or other insulation for winter will suffice.

Propagators Make the Best Gardeners

As I collect and sow seeds or root cuttings from the plants around me, I develop a deeper appreciation and respect for them and a better understanding of their place in this world: In a metaphorical sense, they go from being strangers to friends. Like the Christmas cactus, plants I have multiplied take on a significance in my life far exceeding those I simply picked up fully grown at a local nursery. Like it or not, plant propagation stirs a sort of parental instinct and its concomitant protectiveness, pride, and loyalty.

When I raise a plant up from tenuous infancy to thriving adulthood through trial and error (mostly error!), I learn countless things that help me grow it better in the garden. I learn how its seeds mature and germinate, how quickly it grows, whether it prefers sun or shade, damp conditions or dry, fertile soil or lean. This is why I believe that propagators make the best gardeners—and even if you don't garden and prefer to study plants in the wild, learning to propagate them will teach you much that simple observation cannot.

At the same time, a keen sense of observation will serve you well as a propagator. I have trained many people to propagate plants, but the ones who truly excel—who become the horticultural equivalent of master chef—are those who seem to have an intuitive ability to read plants to determine and even anticipate their wants and needs. Like a superlative sense of taste and smell, this intuition may be something you are born with. Some can do it effortlessly, while others struggle, at least at first. Nevertheless, no matter how good you become at propagation, you will experience your fair share of failures.

A chef can simply toss out a soup that no amount of tweaking has made delicious, but for the propagator, failure inevitably involves killing some plants. When a plant dies, I try to understand where I went wrong, then change soil and temperature, manage pests and diseases, etc., until I get it right. Through simple controlled experimentation, we can unravel many mysteries of plant reproduction.

Propagating Friendships

Looking out over a garden filled with old friends or a ravaged woodland beginning to heal with the help of legions of plants grown under your care gives a satisfaction you can only understand once you have experienced it. A tour around the yard brings a flood of memories of seed-collecting trips, hard-won successes, and places visited. However, one of the most gratifying things about propagating plants is the friendships it fosters among people. Even with a modicum of success, you will soon have more plants than you know what to do with, and there is no better way to win the hearts of plant lovers than to share plants with them. If said plants are rare, unusual, hard-to-find, or uniquely yours, then the effect is amplified exponentially. There's no better way to start a visit, cheer someone up, or thaw the chill after a disagreement than with an offering of plants. Some of my dearest friendships began with the simple sharing of seedlings.

Last year, a friend and remarkable plantswoman passed away after a long fight with cancer. We had become acquainted when she volunteered for me at the nursery, and early on, I gave her some seedlings of a pink-flowered form of showy trillium (*Trillium grandiflorum* var. *roseum*) that I had raised from seeds received from another propagator friend. The plants thrived for a decade or more in her garden, and she told her children before she died that she wanted me to have them. The trilliums are blooming gloriously as I write this and will remind me always of my friend.

My friend started propagating when her children had grown and she finally had some time to herself. By the time I met her 15 years later, she had become quite expert at multiplying some of the most challenging woodland and alpine plants. It is never too late to start propagating! I hope you will give it a try, and I wish you the best of luck. Now, if you will excuse me, I am going to check on my Christmas cactus cuttings.

Stopping Garden Plant Invasions
Sarah Reichard

Imagine a tall herbaceous perennial garden plant with dramatic large leaves and frothy bunches of tiny white flowers in the summer. This handsome plant is tolerant of whatever soil your garden has and needs little or no care. Sounds great, right? Now imagine it has rhizomes (underground stems) that can grow 10 feet deep and extend 24 feet from the mother plant. And that these rhizomes produce dense stands of vegetation that quickly crowd out the other plants in your garden beds, not to mention the lawn and surrounding terrain. If you try to remove the plant and miss a bit of rhizome, the stems can simply travel beneath the soil and pop up in a completely different place, engaging you in a slow-moving plant version of the Whac-a-Mole game. It may even completely disappear for a year or two, then emerge again after you thought it was surely dead. Not so great now, eh?

This plant is not imaginary. In fact, two species of knotweed (*Polygonum*, syn. *Fallopia*)—Japanese knotweed (*P. cuspidatum*) and giant knotweed (*P. sachalinense*)—and their hybrids behave precisely this way. (They can also spread via their prolific, wind-dispersed seeds.) Native to Asia, they are very similar in appearance and have the same detrimental effects. Many gardeners all around the world have been seduced by the charms of these knotweeds and planted them in their gardens, most likely to their eventual regret. I have played Whac-a-Mole with knotweed in my own garden: The plant popped up several feet from where I "killed" it two years before!

As bad as knotweeds can be in your garden, what they do when they invade and colonize wildlands is downright scary. They replace native trees along rivers and streams. Unlike the trees, they are *very* efficient at moving nitrogen from the leaves to the roots in the fall, before dying back. This results in leaf litter that provides far less nutritious food for insects, which means less food for other animals such as the fish that eat the insects. And because of the tenacity of the rhizomes, they nearly always require herbicides for control, another danger to aquatic animals. One species, Japanese knotweed, is considered by the International Union for the Conservation of Nature as one of the 100 worst invasive species—including animals and other types of organisms—worldwide.

Unfortunately, such stories are becoming more common as many other intentionally introduced garden plants jump the garden gate and affect native plants and

Escaped nursery species, like this mile-a-minute vine (*Polygonum perfoliatum*), can wreak havoc in natural areas and threaten native ecosystems.

animals in many harmful ways. More than half of nonnative species that have naturalized in the wild started out as valued garden plants. Some, such as the knotweeds, outcompete native plants, replacing them and altering food webs, soil chemistry, or fire intensity. Nonnative invasive species, including animals, insects, and pathogens, are the second-leading cause of imperilment to endangered species in the United States next to the loss, degradation, and fragmentation of habitat.

Invasive plants not only cause ecological damage, they also cause economic harm. It's very difficult to estimate how much—there are many factors to consider, such as loss of agricultural products, recreational opportunities, and fisheries, as well as the cost of controlling (preventing further spread of) the invasives. David Pimentel, a professor at Cornell University, and his colleagues have conservatively estimated that invasive plants cost the U.S. a stunning $25 billion a year!

Regulation and Control of Pest Plants

One might assume that federal governments screen plants for invasive tendencies prior to allowing them to be imported and sold, but this is done in only a few countries worldwide. The U.S. has recently begun to develop a regulatory framework for such screening, but currently plants are only screened to ensure they don't carry insects or pathogens. The U.S. Department of Agriculture maintains a "noxious weed" list of about 100 species that are invasive but not yet widespread anywhere in the country. (Invasives that are widespread, such as the knotweeds, are regulated at the state level.) It is illegal to sell or transport these species; the emphasis is on preventing an existing invasion from spreading. If a species isn't on this list and the plants are insect and disease free, it's legal to import it.

Many individual states also have noxious weed lists. Some of these are simply advisory—telling the public and nurseries that there is concern about the species but not requiring their control or preventing sale. Western states, and increasingly those in other parts of the country, tend to have lists that are regulatory. A designated state agency, often a department of agriculture, will evaluate a species and determine if it fits its definition of a noxious weed.

Listing a species usually means that it must be controlled, at least in areas of the state where it's not widespread and further spread can be prevented. It may also mean that it cannot be sold in the state, but not all states have such quarantine requirements for all listed noxious weeds. Thus, in some cases, a landowner could be ordered to control a species, while the plant is still being sold at a nursery down the road. Even when a species is quarantined, as knotweeds are in Washington State, they are still sometimes found for sale in nurseries or at plant sales and are traded by gardeners eager to give away something that is becoming too much of a good thing in their gardens.

Even if an invasive species isn't officially listed as a noxious weed, gardeners should refrain from growing them. Native plant societies, universities, botanic gardens, and

Screening Plants for Invasive Tendencies

It would be wonderful if invasive plants demonstrated their wicked ways soon after introduction, but few do. Invasion biologists refer to the period between introduction and invasion as the "lag phase," and it can last several decades for some species. By the time we realize the danger, the plant may be well established. If we want to prevent the introduction of invasive species, we must gain an understanding of the biology of invaders and extrapolate from that—a task to which I've devoted much of my professional career.

I try to use cues from the plants themselves: If a species has characteristics that increase reproduction and/or allow it to tolerate stress, it's more likely to become established and threaten native ecosystems. Among these characteristics are high seed production, ability to begin reproduction early in life, long periods of flowering and fruiting, and ability to spread vegetatively, such as through rhizomes (underground stems).

Vegetative reproduction may allow an invader to not only spread quickly but also escape the stress of disturbance, such as attempted removal: Fragments of rhizomes can survive underground and reestablish new plants. Other stress-tolerant traits include the ability to fix nitrogen (change atmospheric nitrogen into a usable form), which allows a species to populate areas with poor soil nutrition, and green stems, which enables plants to photosynthesize even when they lose their leaves due to cold or drought.

Biologists can apply data on various species traits to formulas that, when analyzed, allow them to predict invasive ability with an acceptable level of accuracy. Because it requires technical knowledge and access to academic publications, it's nearly impossible for most home gardeners to thoroughly assess plants' invasive potential themselves. Fortunately, much information can be found online. Type the name of a species into a search engine along with words like "weed" or "invasive." If you find references to its being a problem in other places with climates similar to yours, it could very well be an invader in your area. (Just be sure to actually read the information—it might be suggesting the species as a safe alternative to another invasive!) Similarly, search for species distribution maps. If a plant is native to a very widespread area in its homeland, this can be an indication that it has invasive abilities—the fact that it has established under various conditions suggests a high degree of stress tolerance and reproductive success.

We've all grown plants that have seeded themselves around our yards. But this propensity alone may not be very informative: Research has found only a moderate correlation between the ability to seed in a garden setting, with its supplemental water and nutrition, and the ability to invade wildlands. However, if a plant demonstrates a number of different invasive traits, then you may have a problem species on your hands. The safest practice is to heed local "do not use" lists and follow the recommendations above to screen for invaders.

How Gardeners Can Help

Following are recommendations for gardeners interested in reducing the damage caused by invasive garden plants in their yards and nearby natural areas, as well as in the larger landscape. The recommendations were developed at the Missouri Botanical Garden in 2001, as part of a workshop aimed at formulating voluntary codes of conduct for the green industry regarding the use of invasive plants.

Seek information on which species are invasive in your area. Sources could include botanic gardens, horticulturists, conservationists, and government agencies. (For example, federal and state noxious weed lists are available on the USDA's online PLANTS Database, plants.usda.gov.) Remove invasive species from your land and replace them with noninvasive species suited to your site and needs.

Ask for only noninvasive species when you acquire plants at a nursery or plant sale, and plant only noninvasive species in your garden. Do not trade plants with other gardeners if you know these species have invasive characteristics.

Request that botanic gardens, nurseries, and garden writers promote, display, and sell only noninvasive species. Politely inform them of the issues—they may not be aware. Urge florists to avoid using invasive species in arrangements; seeds and fruits of invasive plants may be spread via discarded arrangements, and the use of invasives by florists promotes their use among gardeners.

Further knowledge about invasive species by inviting speakers to your garden club, civic group, and neighborhood block association. Speakers can be found in government agencies, colleges, botanic gardens, and conservation organizations.

Seek the best information on the control of invasive plant species and organize neighborhood work groups to remove invasive plant species in your area. Volunteer at botanic gardens and natural areas to learn from knowledgeable professionals while you assist ongoing efforts to diminish the threat of invasive plants. Your parks department almost certainly has such efforts, and volunteering can be a great way to learn about invasives and do a good deed for your community.

Participate in early-warning systems by reporting invasive species you observe in your area. Numerous studies have shown that if an invasive species is detected before it becomes widespread and action is taken, prevention of spread is possible using the least toxic methods, such as removal by hand. Call your local noxious weed program or Cooperative Extension agent; if you're not sure who to contact, inquire at an area botanic garden or college. Local officials may already know about the problem, but it's better to report it than risk having the invasion become too widespread to control.

other entities all produce lists of species that are invasive in a region. Studies have shown that automobiles, birds, and wind are very effective at spreading seeds of invasive plants, so even city gardeners should know that seeds of their plants can find their way beyond urban areas to wildlands. Therefore, if a species is known to be invasive in your area, you should not grow it, regardless of where you live.

Mobilizing Gardeners and the Green Industry

In 2001, I cochaired a workshop at the Missouri Botanical Garden to develop practices that could best prevent the introduction and spread of invasive plant species. Professionals from nurseries and botanic gardens, landscape architects, and amateur gardeners met for three days to discuss how they might be more responsible. Although such voluntary measures are less successful than regulatory actions in removing a species from commerce, they serve as useful tools for education and have allowed an informed conversation to emerge between horticulturists and ecologists.

Attendees at the workshop came up with several recommendations for home gardeners. These included identifying species invasive in your area; removing invasives from your property and replacing them with noninvasive alternatives; and urging local nurseries and florists not to sell regional invasive plants. Botanic gardens took on leadership for education through programs, displays, and partnerships with relevant government agencies.

Composting and Disposing of Invasives

So now you know how to determine your local invasive plants, have removed some from your yard, and are holding them hostage in garden buckets. What to do next? Most invasive plants can be composted. If you compost at home, do not include seeds, because the pile may not get hot enough to kill them, and you'll reseed the plants throughout the garden when you spread the compost. Be careful with rhizomatous plants—as with knotweeds, they may be able to regenerate from a tiny rhizome fragment, and a compost pile is a nice, nutrient-rich place for them to establish, something I learned the hard way. Seeds and rhizomes can be put in the trash. Or even better, put them in a black plastic bag and leave them in the sun for several days until they become mush you can compost.

It's important to remember that while most invasive plants are introduced for garden use, most plants available for garden use are not invasive. There are many beautiful native and noninvasive nonnative species available. My garden has a matrix of native species, with plants from China to Chile mixed in. If something turns out to be invasive and I have to remove it…well, that sounds like a good excuse to go the nursery and buy more, better-behaved plants!

Native Alternatives
for Notorious Invaders

C. Colston Burrell

The lure of the exotic is inescapable. No matter where gardeners live, we are drawn to plants from distant shores. As a result, we often rely on a plant palette that is heavily weighted toward nonnative species, usually those from Europe and Asia. While the vast majority of these horticultural prizes are not invasive, some plants escape cultivation and adapt too well to their adopted shores. They become established, or naturalized, outside of their native range and then proceed to undermine the ecological function of the native ecosystems they invade. Many of these culprits are not universally recognized as invasive exotics; indeed, a plant may be invasive in one region and not in another, or only in a particular soil type within a region.

Exotic invasive species pose a number of problems for native ecosystems. When an invasive establishes in the wild, it displaces a native. Once it becomes entrenched in a native habitat, it begins to proliferate and swamps the native species around it by growing faster, taller, or later into the season, or by leafing out before other species. This rampant intensification of a monoculture transforms the ecosystem, altering hydrology and corrupting nutrient cycles. Invasive shrub or canopy layers also shade out plants on the ground and can inhibit recruitment of new trees that would move the forest to the next successional stage.

In my travels, I keep an eye open for escaped ornamentals that are problematic in various regions. Many of these plants are still seductively marketed to us at our local nurseries, despite their documented ability to degrade ecosystems. The fastest and surest way to stem the rising tide of exotics is for us to stop buying them! Choosing noninvasive alternatives to these pest plants allows us not only to have colorful, beautiful, and ecologically sustainable gardens but also to forge stronger links with local ecosystems.

Selecting Alternatives 101

Plants satisfy diverse desires in the varied settings within our gardens. They form the permanent as well as the ephemeral structure that defines boundaries and spaces. Trees, shrubs, and herbaceous perennials contribute form, color, and texture with

The Sputnik-like, fragrant inflorescences of native buttonbush (*Cephalanthus occidentalis*) are a hit with pollinators, making it a great alternative for invasive butterfly bush (*Buddleja davidii*).

Checklist for Choosing Alternatives

- ✓ Is the plant regionally native?
- ✓ Will the plant thrive in your hardiness zone and site conditions?
- ✓ Does the plant bloom at the desired time of year?
- ✓ Are the flowers or fruit the desired color?
- ✓ Is the inflorescence the desired shape and size?
- ✓ Is the foliage similar in form, texture, and color to that of the invasive?
- ✓ Is the overall shape and size of the plant similar?
- ✓ Does the plant have multiple seasons of interest?
- ✓ Is the root system similar?
- ✓ Is the plant easy to establish and maintain?

their flowers, foliage, fruits, and bark. Most of us are drawn to flowers—the most flamboyant attribute—first. Foliage is the most enduring and compelling characteristic during the growing season; myriad shades of green in varied shapes and sizes carry the garden. Colorful and shapely fruits and seedheads are seductive, especially when the garden is winding down for the year; distinctive bark and branching patterns are especially alluring when the garden is dormant in winter.

When you've been seduced by an invasive and would like to find a native alternative, consider the attributes of the plant—such as color, form, and texture—that appealed to you in the first place. Then narrow your choice by thinking locally and considering your site conditions. Is your alternative choice native to your region? Will it thrive in the soil and exposure of the site? Try to match the features that attracted you to the invasive plant: color, seasonality, overall shape, and size. Ease of care is also critically important: An alternative that needs coddling to succeed will never catch on as a viable substitute for a tough stalwart.

Here's an example of how it works. Linden viburnum (*Viburnum dilatatum*), a beloved but aggressive invasive ornamental in mid- to late-successional forests, is prized for its domed, creamy-white flower clusters, decorative red fruits, burgundy autumn color, and rounded form. As substitutions, you could choose from a variety of native species that convey the overall look. The closest match for eastern gardeners is red chokeberry (*Photinia pyrifolia*), whose luminous red fruits develop from clustered white flowers. The elongated oval leaves are burgundy to crimson in autumn, and the form ranges from rounded to upright oval. Myriad native viburnums are also available, though most have blue or black fruits rather than red. Trade-offs are sometimes necessary, but for most potentially invasive ornamentals, you should be able to find a number of locally native alternatives that closely match.

Following are profiles of a few common offenders in the U.S. and some fantastic natives to plant instead. The alternatives listed represent the closest matches that could be made based on color and shape of flowers, foliage, and fruits, as well as architectural attributes such as overall form. For more in-depth information as well as many additional profiles, see the Brooklyn Botanic Garden handbooks *Great Natives for Tough Places* and *Native Alternatives to Invasive Plants*, and on the web, visit the PlantWise invasive-to-native translator tool (beplantwise.org/tools/alternatives.php).

Flowers First

Flowers seduce us with stimulating color, remarkable shapes, and alluring fragrance, attributes that often motivate the choice of plants for the garden.

INVADER Butterfly Bush
SOME ALTERNATIVES Buttonbush, Sweet Pepperbush, Ceanothus

Ceanothus cuneatus

Colorful, fragrant, summer-blooming butterfly bush (*Buddleja davidii*) is aptly named for its ability to attract lepidopterans, but it readily colonizes gravelly soils, rock outcroppings, and other tough sites across the U.S. Eastern gardeners can eschew this aggressive self-seeder from China for the native buttonbush (*Cephalanthus occidentalis*), whose comically Sputnik-like, fragrant white inflorescences are mobbed by butterflies and other pollinators in summer. Another excellent butterfly magnet with summer flowers is sweet pepperbush (*Clethra alnifolia*). In the West, chose one of the many *Ceanothus* species, which produce intensely fragrant flower clusters in white or stunning shades of blue.

INVADER Callery Pear
SOME ALTERNATIVES Serviceberry, Hawthorn

Amelanchier laevis

The snowy flowers of Callery pear (*Pyrus calleryana*), an Asian native, open early in the season. They festoon weak-wooded cultivars such as 'Bradford', which can dramatically self-destruct in high winds and icy conditions. Like General Sherman's march to the sea, seedlings from these cultivars are cutting a destructive swath across the South. They form impenetrable thickets in fields, along woodland borders, and on highway verges. Instead of this invader, try an airy serviceberry (*Amelanchier* species) for early white flowers and red-orange autumn foliage, or the green hawthorn cultivar *Crataegus viridis* 'Winter King', a disease-resistant selection that bears profuse clusters of white flowers in May.

Fabulous Foliage

Many of our most familiar foliage plants are exotic—and some of them are notorious invaders. Our native flora offers a wealth of underutilized plants with colorful summer and autumn foliage that can be used in their stead.

INVADER English Ivy

SOME ALTERNATIVES Salal, Western Wild Ginger, Carolina Jessamine

English ivy (*Hedera helix*) provides a serviceable carpet of green foliage year-round, but it's as outdated as a shag rug. It covers every horizontal and vertical surface it encounters, and it's an invasive on both coasts. Alternatives for eastern and mid-Atlantic gardens include

Gaultheria shallon

bigleaf aster (*Eurybia macrophylla*) and barren strawberry, and if the soil is sandy, bearberry (*Arctostaphylos uva-ursi*). Western gardeners can substitute native groundcovers such as Cascade barberry (*Mahonia nervosa*), salal (*Gaultheria shallon*), and western wild ginger (*Asarum caudatum*). Those in the Southeast can use Allegheny spurge (*Pachysandra procumbens*) as an alternative. For vertical coverage, plant a climbing vine like white-flowered wood vamp (*Decumaria barbara*), orange crossvine (*Bignonia capreolata*), yellow Carolina jessamine (*Gelsemium sempervirens*) in the Southeast, or orange honeysuckle (*Lonicera ciliosa*) in the West.

Bountiful Berries

Many of our worst invasive plants spread from bountiful berries carried afar by birds and beasts, or from seeds blown alee by the wind.

INVADER Heavenly Bamboo

SOME ALTERNATIVES Florida Hobblebush, Yaupon, Manzanita

With its glossy evergreen foliage and scarlet late-season berries, heavenly bamboo (*Nandina domestica*) is a darling of the landscaping industry. But across the south and in California, this mainstay from India and eastern Asia is invading forests, open woods, and

Ilex vomitoria

savannas. Birds and small mammals like mice scatter the fruits far beyond the garden gate. For native alternatives with evergreen foliage and an arching habit, try Florida hobblebush (*Agarista populifolia*) or fetterbush (*Lyonia lucida*). For similar bright red berries, try hollies like yaupon (*Ilex vomitoria*) or dahoon (*Ilex cassine*). California gardeners should consider red-fruited toyon (*Heteromeles arbutifolia*), evergreen manzanita (*Arctostaphylos* species), or ceanothus.

Branch and Bark

The architectural shapes and patterns of woody plants are among their most alluring attributes. Whether exfoliating, rough and furrowed, or smooth and glossy, bark features prominently in our attraction to trees and shrubs.

INVADER Privet
SOME ALTERNATIVES Wax Myrtle, Yaupon, Bayberry

Morella cerifera

Privet (*Ligustrum* species) is still favored as a cheap and fast-growing hedge or screen. All species (whether of Asian or European origin) are documented escapers, no doubt eager to be free of constant clipping. They clog stream corridors and floodplains all across the U.S., growing as impenetrable green walls that eliminate all competition. Good substitutes should be evergreen, compact, and reasonably fine-textured. In warmer regions along the Atlantic and Gulf of Mexico, choose southern wax myrtle (*Morella cerifera*), yaupon (*Ilex vomitoria*), or buckwheat tree (*Cliftonia monophylla*). In cooler zones, consider inkberry (*Ilex glabra*), which is glossy and dense, as is northern bayberry (*Morella pensylvanica*). In the West, choose mountain mahogany (*Cercocarpus* species), manzanita, toyon, coffeeberry (*Frangula californica*), or ceanothus.

A Glimmer of Hope

Although the exotic invasives mentioned here and many other plants continue to threaten our native ecosystems, the source of the problem in gardens and nurseries is improving. Education works. Word is spreading, and some invasive plants, once readily available, are vanishing from the nursery trade. Amur honeysuckle (*Lonicera maackii*), autumn olive (*Elaeagnus umbellata*), and ice plant (*Carpobrotus edulis*) may remain problematic in the wild, but they are seldom offered for sale anymore. With time, I predict that the rest of the plants on my list will vanish from the trade as well (though we must always remain vigilant in our efforts to screen new introductions for invasive tendencies). Our gardens can be beautiful and colorful without invasive plants, and the more regionally native species we establish, the more we do to protect and restore our local ecosystems.

Connections with Native Plants

Mariellé Anzelone

Connections are easy for people to make in a city. Without much ado, we can catch a train, make a call, bump into a friend on the street, log onto wireless internet. This is no accident—urban centers are designed with the infrastructure and density to support these convenient interactions. At any time, we can tap into a larger grid created to support our individual lifestyles.

But that's the human point of view. No doubt a wildflower would feel differently. If it could talk, what would the bloodroot's opinion be of the urban environment? Our native *Sanguinaria canadensis* would probably say that far from making things easier, the design of cities has impeded its way of life. With populations dwindling in the city landscape, bloodroot is having a hard time keeping up with human activity.

It's perplexing that we seem determined to banish bloodroot from the places where we live, because it is lovely to behold. This spring ephemeral appears just after snowmelt in early spring. As it emerges, the plant pierces through newly thawed soil. It pushes upward with its single leaf wrapped protectively around its single flower bud. Once safely aboveground, the bud expands to reveal a large, porcelain-white blossom. The flower is a fleeting presence, usually lasting only two days—but those two days are pure delight. Eight to ten brilliant-white petals radiate outward from a golden-yellow center. The open floral architecture welcomes pollinators and also invites humans in for a closer look.

A Busy Little Wildflower

Each year, bloodroot's top goal is to create progeny. As an early-spring bloomer, it faces a number of obstacles to pollination, including a short blooming season that overlaps with the flowering of other species. Then there's the lack of pollinators. Limited hours, bad weather, option paralysis over where to eat—these things that keep New Yorkers in on a Friday night also influence pollinator activity. We can hardly blame the long-tongued bees, syrphid flies, and bumble bees, especially in an urban environment, where they must traverse an often unfriendly landscape to reap their nectar rewards. Thankfully, bloodroot has a backup plan. After thousands of years of evolution, encoded deep within the plant's DNA is a strategy for dealing with the vagaries of weather and unreliable pollinators—self-pollination.

The author's native plant garden in New York City's Union Square Park draws birds, bees, and butterflies; models sustainable park design; and brings urbanites a little closer to nature.

On day three after opening, if insect pollination hasn't occurred, the flower essentially tires of waiting for visitors and pollinates itself. After fertilization, seeds develop inside an elongated green pod. Each seed has a fatty appendage attached to it. These elaiosomes attract woodland ant species that carry the booty back to their nests. Here, the fat bodies are consumed and the unharmed seeds are thrown into the garbage heap, a rich compost that stimulates germination.

Ant-transported seeds don't travel far—they don't need to. Since the current location is favorable for the parent plant, it should suit its progeny as well. The assumption of myrmecochory, or seed dispersal by ants, is that the habitat is stable and constant. One study showed the seeds of a woodland wildflower moving only 100 yards over a 1,000-year period. Such locally dispersed seeds could bear a bumper sticker asking, "Why mess with success?"

Struggling in a Fragmented Landscape

You know how this story ends. Humans, of course, do mess with success, disrupting this mutually beneficial ant-plant relationship. The rich, mesic (moist) forests that bloodroot calls home make excellent sites for "civic improvements" like ball fields, public works projects, and parkways. This change in land-use status away from forest ecosystems destroys on-site plants outright and leaves adjacent populations neighborless and isolated.

Some species can dance around the urban landscape unimpeded. Many aster family species sport plumes that alight and disperse on the wind. Some rose family species produce fruits that are eaten and deposited by birds. But ants can't cross a road. The seeds of bloodroot are stymied by urbanization, and the plant will most likely never evolve to cope with pressures like habitat fragmentation.

The impact of this legacy of land use can be seen throughout the city. Although bloodroot populations are still found in three of the five boroughs (the Bronx, Queens, and Staten Island), *Sanguinaria canadensis* is on the decline. The number of occurrences has dwindled, and recruitment (the establishment of new plants) is low. Worse still, bloodroot is not alone in this struggle. Myrmecochory is a common strategy among native woodland herbs, including wild ginger (*Asarum canadense*), *Trillium* species, and twinleaf (*Jeffersonia diphylla*). Sensitivity to habitat fragmentation makes these species excellent gauges of the health of an ecosystem but also leaves them vulnerable. After a disturbance, it may take decades for their slow-growing colonies to reappear—if they return at all.

An Urban Planning Oversight

High-quality habitats—including parkland—are continuously destroyed, and there are often no policies in place to protect them. For example, despite its "forever wild" designation, Four Sparrow Marsh in Brooklyn is presently on offer to developers. The site constitutes some of the last salt marsh in the city. Smaller development projects within parks also erode the store of biodiversity therein: the ball field situated in a swamp forest or the nature center built atop locally rare grasses.

Poor management practices are also to blame. Active recreational pursuits like mountain biking are permitted in sensitive natural areas. Police direct all-terrain vehicle users to parks. With no perimeter barriers to stop them, these vehicles gain access to and tear up the herbaceous layer of our woodlands. Few resources are available for conservation and rare species retention. Sites are allowed to decline until intensive restoration becomes the only answer. But restoration requires a significant financial investment, and only a limited number of grants are available.

Less than one percent of New York City's budget goes toward parks. And the money the Parks and Recreation department does receive is mostly allocated to recreational uses. Despite the amount of open space involved—green spaces make up nearly one-eighth of the area of the city—parks are not viewed as worthy of investment. They are mostly overlooked, as is the Big Apple's status as the city with the most nature (25,000 acres) in North America.

It's partly a case of out of sight, out of mind, because most city legislators and residents don't set foot in their parks at all. In the creation of New York City, natural areas were something of an afterthought. As Manhattan of the mid-1800s grew more populous, city planners looked to the island's northern tip and the Bronx for undeveloped land to preserve. Most open space in Brooklyn, Queens, and Staten Island was set aside decades later. The result is a hodgepodge of sites of varying sizes, quality, and locations. Today much of the mix of city, state, and federal parkland is located at the city's fringes, out of reach of mass transit and hard for people to get to.

That said, New York's natural heritage has a surprisingly large fan base. Residents are hungry to hear about this other, greener side of their city. Sadly, few resources are available, and in general, people are unable to connect with wild plants. Charismatic wild animals and cultivated garden plants are capable of fascinating and holding folks' attention. But there is little understanding and no constituency of support around the naturally occurring flora that is a critical part of the city's ecological viability.

Rebuilding Connectivity Among Plants, Animals, and People

Lack of knowledge and advocacy don't have to stand as the status quo. If city residents are given both the opportunity and the context to connect with nature, change can occur—change that's better for people, plants, and the animals plants support.

This is the inspiration behind NYC Wildflower Week (nycwildflowerweek.org), an annual spring event I cofounded to encourage New Yorkers of all ages to explore and help protect the natural heritage of the city. Activities include guided botanical walks through New York's woodlands and wetlands, tours of native gardens and green roofs, native plant workshops and giveaways, and interactive children's fairs.

During my tenure as a plant ecologist for the city, I also created the native plant display garden in Union Square Park in lower Manhattan. Hundreds of people pass it daily at Union Square West and East 15th Street. Local plant communities inspired its design, and it showcases New York native wildflowers, ferns, shrubs, and grasses. Matching these perennials to site conditions resulted in a low-maintenance, resource-saving floristic display. For example, wet and sunny garden sections have plants typically found in freshwater marshes, while areas of shade and moderate soil moisture feature forest flora.

Conceived and designed in 2006, the garden achieves a number of goals simultaneously—it educates New Yorkers by engaging them with their foliar neighbors; it serves as a habitat haven for birds, bees, and butterflies; it models sustainable ecological design in public parks; and it encourages place-based nature education in schools.

Unfortunately, these and other initiatives for connecting people with nature have been slow to gain traction in New York City, at least at the official level: With little policy recognition of the importance of our natural heritage and its stewardship, the city sometimes seems to be in the biodiversity Dark Ages.

The Union Square native plant garden is a step toward enlightenment. Situated in a public space near a major transportation hub, its accessibility and scale encourage visitor intimacy with the plants. There is no forest, grassland, or marsh remaining in this part of Manhattan, so the Union Square native plant garden fills a vital biological role as well. This 2,400-square-foot patch of habitat restores local biodiversity, providing certain animals with a stepping-stone or stopover habitat on their way to visiting the city's larger green spaces and preserves. I've found monarch caterpillars and spicebush swallowtails in the garden, insects that rely on certain native plants as their sole food source. The space also creates a visual and psychological link for another species starved for an organic connection to place and to the services that nature provides—*Homo sapiens.*

Bringing It Home

In our urbanized world, the concept of cities as "concrete jungles" is inaccurate and serves only to alienate people from the natural world. Conserving, maintaining, and expanding the ecosystems on which cities depend are essential to the health, well-being, and quality of life of their citizens. Since more people now live in cities than in rural areas around the globe, our urban designs and educational endeavors need to bridge the gaps—both real and perceived—between humans and local nature more effectively than ever before.

Conservation education without local context may actually reinforce feelings of alienation from nature. For example, in a recent campaign for polar bears promoted in many schools, children learned important information about the sad plight of a charismatic species thousands of miles away. It is unlikely they heard anything about the rare salamander or spider—much less the endangered plant—that's hanging on for dear life in their own neighborhood. Localized nature education can address this, helping people feel connected to the place where they live. In addition to fostering civic engagement, such instruction can provide enormous benefits for individuals and society.

Play in nature has been shown to increase children's emotional capacity, problem-solving ability, creativity, self-esteem, and self-discipline. It can also be excellent therapy for depression, obesity, and attention deficit disorder. For adults, a walk in the forest lowers stress, increases cognitive function, and boosts immune cells that fight cancer.

Nature-based activities can also nurture social and emotional connections among people. For instance, volunteering to help clean up a local creek or restore a neighborhood park helps build community among city residents, giving them a shared sense of camaraderie and purpose as stewards of biodiversity.

Gardens as Green Corridors

In New York City, despite the relative abundance of natural areas, the "nature for nature's sake" viewpoint doesn't exist. City planners don't strategically consider plants with ant-dispersed seeds. But maybe they should. Bloodroot's perspective of habitat fragmentation and loss can teach us something. Are we really planning cities for the benefit of people when we don't take the needs of bloodroot and other species into account? What do we lose when only expediency and economics are considered?

From a conservation standpoint, small connective stepping-stones like the native plant garden in Union Square Park only benefit a particular suite of fauna or flora—those that are highly mobile, or that depend on mobile species for pollination or dispersal. While supporting these plants and animals is of crucial importance, some species need a deep dark woods or an expansive grassland in order to persist. Building a narrow patchwork of biodiversity won't help bloodroot and other organisms in the same boat. Only large continuous tracts of land will do. Still, small patches of green space can nevertheless help build support among the populace for the preservation of the larger open spaces needed to help these species.

Imagine streetscapes rich with life: large street tree pits filled with wildflowers, grasses, and ferns. Imagine city backyards, rooftop gardens, patio planters, and window boxes teeming with native flora. In these native plant patches would be places for pollinators to alight and feed or reproduce, and for people to meet their human and botanical neighbors. We can all contribute to this vision, no matter the size of our gardens or budgets.

Even more can be done to support local flora. See it firsthand by going for a walk in the woods with a field book or human guide. Join a botanical society. Write letters to your local and state representatives in support of the preservation of open space near you. By recognizing and fostering the relationship between city and nature, we nurture our human connection to it and to each other.

The Native Flora Garden

Uli Lorimer

As I stroll through the two-acre Native Flora Garden at Brooklyn Botanic Garden (BBG) and marvel at the beautiful landscape, I sometimes think about the rich histories—cultural and botanical—that are layered underneath. A haven for native plant communities in the heart of a dense metropolis, the garden—which celebrated its centenary in 2011—was not long ago the site of an open grassland dotted with the livestock that supported the nearby communities and settlements. In precolonial times, the scene would have been much different.

Few New Yorkers today can imagine what the metropolitan area looked like prior to European settlement. Mention the New Jersey Meadowlands, for instance, and most folks think mob hits, garbage dumps, industrial parks, and mile upon mile of invasive nonnative *Phragmites* grass. But the Meadowlands were once the site of an extensive Atlantic white cedar (*Chamaecyparis thyoides*) swamp, ringed by salt marshes and dotted with freshwater *Sphagnum* bogs containing sundews (*Drosera* species), pitcher plants (*Sarracenia* species), and fringed orchids (*Platanthera* species). Instead of freeways, housing, and airport runways, pitch pine (*Pinus rigida*) and oak (*Quercus* species) forests once surrounded Jamaica Bay, and where JFK International Airport sits, thousands of dragon's-mouth orchids (*Arethusa bulbosa*) once grew. One of only a few naturally occurring prairie ecosystems on the east coast of the United States, the Hempstead Plains graced nearly 60,000 acres of what is now suburban Long Island. These are just some of the botanical treasures lost to development and urban expansion, much of it within the last 100 years or so.

In the early 20th century, as advances in transportation and technology boosted urban development, most New Yorkers were oblivious to the environmental destruction going on within and at the fringes of their city. Terms like "habitat loss," "species extinction," and "conservation" were not part of the everyday lexicon. However, local botanists and plant lovers recognized the threats faced by native flora. Stuart Gager and Norman Taylor, the first director and curator of plants at BBG, respectively, were among them.

Before Taylor joined BBG in 1910 (the year the Garden opened to the public), he had spent years in the field as a research taxonomist, studying local native plants

BBG's pioneering Native Flora Garden offers a living diorama of local plant communities, serving the parallel goals for education and conservation.

and classifying their relationships. His interest in local plant communities played an influential part in BBG's prescient decision, in 1911, to open a garden dedicated to the display, study, and conservation of local New York flora.

Early Layout and Conservation Efforts

Situated in the northwestern corner of Brooklyn Botanic Garden, the Local Flora Section, as it was initially called, was first planted as a wildflower garden and woodland. The design was twofold: Groves of trees and shrubs were installed in the north end with the express purpose of creating genuine woodland conditions through the gradual maturation of the woody plants; at the south end, wildflower beds were laid out in systematic fashion—that is, arranged according to plant family and evolutionary relationships.

Herbaceous plants were displayed in beds so that Taylor could easily conduct classification studies as well as research into flower pollination and seed dispersal. Taylor's research not only influenced the design but also the plant selection. Plants grown in the garden were from wild-collected sources rather than from nursery stock. This is standard operation in today's conservation gardens, but in Taylor's time, few natives were commercially available, so he had no choice but to collect species from the wild and propagate them for use in the garden. In any case, Taylor also recognized that wild-collected plants were better adapted for handling local environmental stresses than commercially produced material.

From the beginning, the Local Flora Section supported plant conservation efforts through seed collection, propagation, and reintroduction. For example, in 1926, resident investigator Ralph Curtiss Benedict wrote in BBG's *Garden Record* about ongoing efforts with the rare hart's tongue fern (*Asplenium scolopendrium* var. *americanum*):

> "The program for the conservation of native plants endangered by industrial and park expansion, etc., has required a considerable amount of attention. Spore cultures of hart's tongue fern, started in 1925, were brought along to potting size by early summer of 1926 and, according to plans earlier announced, distribution was made of these young plants for the purpose of naturalization. Plants were sent to 16 different people distributed in 8 different states, with the distinct understanding that the ferns were to be set out under conditions as nearly like their natural habitat as possible and those to whom the plants were sent were asked to keep close watch of them, so as to report the success of this broad demonstration experiment."

The *Garden Record* also reveals that many other plants now considered regionally threatened or endangered were being grown in the Local Flora Section, including *Corema conradii* (Conrad's crowberry), *Helonias bullata* (swamp-pink), *Schizaea pusilla* (curly grass fern), and several species of orchids.

A Pioneering Ecological Design

In the decade following the creation of the Local Flora Section, Taylor became more interested in plant ecology than systematics, focusing his research on plant communities and ecological relationships on Long Island. He once declared that floristic inventories were "as necessary and uninteresting as the telephone directory." In 1929, plans were announced to redevelop the Local Flora Section, discontinuing the arrangement of herbaceous plants in beds and instead organizing the garden along ecological lines.

Much of the credit for the design of the new garden, completed in 1931, lay with assistant curator of plants Henry Knute Svenson. In the words of Gager, "[Svenson] has worked out a plan for an ecological treatment, so that…not only are the local… trees, shrubs, and herbaceous plants exhibited, but the subject of the relation of plants to their environment is also illustrated."

In BBG's 1931 annual report, Svenson called the redesign "an attempt to preserve a bit of country in urban surroundings," explaining, "The beds, which were the feature of this area, have been entirely obliterated and their place has been taken by habitat areas, each designed to represent some outstanding feature of vegetation to be found within one hundred miles of New York. Little has been done in the region of New York to preserve the unique habitats which are required by many species, and as a consequence some of our most interesting wild plants are doomed so far as growth in the vicinity of a large city is concerned, the chief adverse factors being the cutting of woodlands and the draining of swamps and bogs."

One of the first ecologically themed native plant gardens of its kind in the U.S., the revamped Local Flora Section highlighted nine plant communities found in the Northeast: serpentine rock, dry meadow, kettle pond, bog, pine barrens, wet meadow and stream, deciduous woodland, limestone ledge, and coniferous forest. Accuracy and authenticity of the display was a major concern for Svenson. He also felt it was important that the garden re-create the atmosphere of a true wilderness. Using wild-collected plants from each of the nine distinct habitats, he developed an exhibit that allowed visitors to have an accurate, immersive encounter with nature without having to leave the city.

The Mature Garden

As the current curator of this garden, I am privileged to continue the efforts set in motion by Taylor, Svenson, and others. The Native Flora Garden, as it's called today, has an almost magical authenticity as you stroll along its paths, due in large part to its age. The trees planted in the early days have matured into a collection of giants, some towering 100 feet or more over the forest floor. The leaves, seeds, and branches of these trees have contributed to nearly a century of soil formation, creating ideal conditions for shade-loving ferns and wildflowers.

BBG is a custodian of pixie moss (*Pyxidanthera barbulata*), a locally threatened species.

Future Conservation Efforts

BBG is undertaking a two-acre expansion of the Native Flora Garden. Roughly one acre will be dedicated to meadow habitat, using a plant palette derived from the remnant grasslands of Hempstead Plains, on Long Island, and the serpentine barrens of Staten Island. The remaining acre will be used to display pine barrens habitat. A pond and surrounding shore area will feature typical lowland and wetland pine barrens vegetation, while dry sandy areas surrounding the pond will become home to upland plant communities dominated by pitch pine and various oaks. The plant material for this new garden will come entirely from locally collected seeds of wild plants.

The garden expansion will provide ample opportunity to develop BBG's conservation program. The current lack of appropriate habitat is restricting the Garden's efforts to cultivate and monitor plants propagated from wild-collected seed for in situ (on-site) conservation. Due to their unique conditions, both the pine barrens and serpentine barrens of the New York metropolitan region are home to many of the threatened and endangered flora of the region.

Brooklyn Botanic Garden, in collaboration with the Center for Plant Conservation, serves as custodian of five locally threatened species: sensitive joint vetch (*Aeschynomene virginica*), bog asphodel (*Narthecium americanum*), pixie moss (*Pyxidanthera barbulata*), American chaffseed (*Schwalbea americana*), and Knieskern's beaksedge (*Rynchospora knieskernii*), all of which can be found only in pine barrens ecosystems. With an expanded Native Flora Garden, BBG can design new research initiatives to investigate propagation, pollination, dispersal, and genetic fitness of these and other endangered native plants to ensure that they are not lost, as so many other regionally native plants have been.

The garden continues to fulfill the three parallel roles intended by its founders and carried forward by subsequent gardeners and curators: display, education, and conservation. The Native Flora Garden is an example of a naturalistic, ecologically based exhibit that allows visitors the experience of a walk in the woods. It also continues to be an important resource for on-site conservation and research. Biodiversity is being lost from our wild areas at a frightening pace, and gardens like the Native Flora Garden provide a crucial resource for propagation, pollination, and dispersal research. Furthermore, the garden serves as a genetic repository and long-term seed bank for threatened species, ensuring their survival in cultivation at the very least.

The Native Flora Garden enjoys a close relationship with the department of Science at BBG, which has been conducting a multiyear study of the flora of New York City and its surrounding environment (see "The Metropolitan Flora," page 18). Through repeated field trips into the wild areas of the region, BBG botanists have located populations of threatened plants and collected their seeds, which in turn have been propagated and brought into cultivation in the Native Flora Garden. By growing these plants in a garden setting, we can show the public what is being lost and why. We are also using and preserving local genotypes, an important practice not just with endangered plants but with all new introductions into the garden. Locally collected seed-grown natives are adapted to our growing conditions and contain broad genetic diversity, which increases their chances of coping with future challenges, such as climate change.

The last, and perhaps most important, function of the Native Flora Garden is to continue exposing generations of children and adults to the diversity and splendor of New York's native plant communities. In our increasingly urbanized world, people have fewer and fewer chances to encounter authentic wildness and nature; in New York City, BBG's native garden is helping many folks, especially kids, make that important connection.

As the Native Flora Garden heads into its second century, a major challenge looms large: The tree canopy has matured, shading out sun-loving plant communities like the pine barrens, the serpentine barrens, and meadows. We simply don't have the cultural conditions to display these plants well. A garden expansion, scheduled to begin in 2012, will allow us to breathe new life into the declining exhibits. It will also give us the opportunity to improve the educational experience for our visitors. The Native Flora Garden has much to teach about plant communities and the environment; the interactions between plants, insects and wildlife; the importance of native plants as they relate to our natural, cultural, and economic heritage; and the vital importance of conservation efforts that support biodiversity.

The future of the garden is bright and full of hope. It has been an inspiration for our visitors over the last century and will continue to shine well into the next.

For More Information

NATIVE PLANT RESOURCES

Center for Plant Conservation
centerforplantconservation.org
Nonprofit organization dedicated to
conserving and restoring rare native plants
of the U.S.

GardenWeb Native Plants Forum
forums.gardenweb.com/forums/natives/
Connect with native plant enthusiasts for
growing tips, recommendations, and more.

Lady Bird Johnson Wildflower Center
wildflower.org/plants
Native plant database, searchable by
state, growing conditions, and physical
characteristics.

New England Wild Flower Society
newfs.org
Articles and videos on growing and
conserving native plants.

North American Native Plant Society
nanps.org
Information on cultivation and restoration
of native plants, plus a native plant society
directory.

PlantNative
plantnative.org
Nationwide directory of native plant
nurseries and regional plant lists
searchable by state.

USDA Plants Database
plants.usda.gov
Native plant distribution maps searchable
by species and state.

Wild Ones
www.for-wild.org
Nonprofit organization promoting
the preservation, restoration, and
establishment of native plant communities.

EARLY PLANT COLLECTORS

*Pioneer Naturalists: The Discovery
and Naming of North American Plants
and Animals*
Howard Ensign Evans, Henry Holt and
Company, 1993

NATIVE PLANT SEED COLLECTING

**USDA Forest Service
National Seed Laboratory**
nsl.fs.fed.us
Information on harvesting seeds from
woody plants and genetic conservation of
native plants.

*Collecting, Processing,
and Germinating Seeds of
Wildland Plants*
James A. Young and Cheryl G. Young,
Timber Press, 1986

ECOLOGICAL RESTORATION IN THE GARDEN

*Gardening with a Wild Heart:
Restoring California's Native
Landscapes at Home*
Judith Larner Lowry, University of California
Press, 2000

*The Landscaping Ideas of Jays:
A Natural History of the Backyard
Restoration Garden*
Judith Larner Lowry, University of California
Press, 2007

*Noah's Garden: Restoring the
Ecology of Our Own Backyards*
Sarah Stein, Houghton Mifflin, 1993

BBG BOOKS ON NATIVE PLANTS

Great Natives for Tough Places
Niall Dunne, editor, 2009

Native Alternatives to Invasive Plants
C. Colston Burrell, Janet Marinelli, Bonnie Harper-Lore, editors, 2006

Wildflower Gardens
C. Colston Burrell, editor, 1999

Native Perennials
Nancy Beaubaire, editor, 1996

Going Native
Janet Marinelli, editor, 1994

WELCOMING WILDLIFE

Bringing Nature Home: How You Can Sustain Wildlife with Native Plants
Douglas W. Tallamy, Timber Press, 2007

The Wildlife Gardeners Guide
Janet Marinelli, Brooklyn Botanic Garden, 2008

Attracting Native Pollinators: Protecting North Americas Bees and Butterflies
The Xerces Society, Storey Publishing, 2011

National Wildlife Federation Garden for Wildlife Program
http://www.nwf.org/Get-Outside/Outdoor-Activities/Garden-for-Wildlife.aspx
Detailed information on how to create and certify a wildlife habitat garden.

The Xerces Society
www.xerces.org
Information about invertebrates and conservation of their habitats.

EDIBLE NATIVE PLANTS

Wild Plants I Have Known and Eaten
Russ Cohen, Essex County Greenbelt Association, 2004

Nature's Garden: A Guide to Indentifying, Harvesting, and Preparing Edible Wild Plants
Samuel Thayer, Forager's Harvest Press, 2010

NATIVE PLANT PROPAGATION

Wildflowers: A Guide to Growing and Propagating Native Flowers of North America
William Cullina, Houghton Mifflin Harcourt, 2000

Native Trees, Shrubs, and Vines: A Guide to Using, Growing, and Propagating North American Woody Plants
William Cullina, Houghton Mifflin Harcourt, 2002

Native Plant Network Propagation Protocol Database
nativeplantnetwork.org/Network
Technical information on to how to propagate North American natives, searchable by plant name.

INVASIVE PLANTS

Invasive Plants
John M. Randall and Janet Marinelli, editors, Brooklyn Botanic Garden, 1996

Invasive and Exotic Species of North America
www.invasive.org
Information on identifying and controlling invasive plants and animals; includes an invasive plant atlas of the U.S.

Contributors

Mariellé Anzelone is an urban conservation biologist whose work as a garden designer, lecturer, and writer aims to connect New Yorkers to the nature around them. She is the founder of NYC Wildflower Week and a contributor to the *New York Times*.

Myla Aronson is an assistant professor of biology at Hofstra University. She holds an MS and PhD in ecology and evolution from Rutgers University and a BS in natural resources from Cornell University. Her research focuses on the patterns and drivers of biodiversity in human-dominated landscapes, and on how to conserve and restore this biodiversity.

C. Colston Burrell is an acclaimed lecturer, garden designer, writer, and photographer. The author of 12 garden books, he is a popular lecturer internationally on topics of design, plants, and ecology. He is also principal of Native Landscape Design and Restoration, which specializes in blending nature and culture through artistic design.

Russ Cohen is an environmentalist and wild foods enthusiast and the author of *Wild Plants I Have Known...and Eaten* (Essex County Greenbelt Association, 2004). He serves as the rivers advocate for the Division of Ecological Restoration at the Massachusetts Department of Fish and Game. He has also taught edible wild plant and mushroom courses throughout New England for more than 30 years.

William Cullina is the acting executive director for the Coastal Maine Botanical Gardens, in Boothbay, Maine. A well-known author and recognized authority on North American native plants, he lectures on a variety of subjects to garden and professional groups and writes for popular and technical journals. His books include *Wildflowers* and *Native Trees, Shrubs, and Vines* (Houghton Mifflin Harcourt, 2000 and 2002, respectively).

Niall Dunne is a former staff editor at Brooklyn Botanic Garden and the editor of BBG's handbooks *Great Natives for Tough Places* (2009) and *Healthy Soil for Sustainable Gardens* (2009). He holds an MA in English from University College Dublin and an MS in ecology from Rutgers University. He lives in Seattle and manages publications and communications for the Arboretum Foundation at Washington Park Arboretum.

Steven Glenn is manager of the New York Metropolitan Flora Project at Brooklyn Botanic Garden. He has conducted floristic research in the New York–New Jersey–Connecticut region for the past 17 years, with a focus on creating detailed distribution maps for all regional vascular plant species.

Bernd Heinrich is professor emeritus in the Department of Biology at the University of Vermont. He is the author of more than 15 books, including *The Trees in My Forest* and *Bumblebee Economics*. He is also the subject of a recent documentary, *An Uncommon Curiosity: At Home and in Nature with Bernd Heinrich*.

Wendy Hollender is a botanical artist, instructor, and author whose work has been widely exhibited and published. Her latest book is *Botanical Drawing in Color: A Basic Guide to Mastering Realistic Form and Naturalistic Color* (Random House, 2010). She lives and works in Ulster County, New York (drawingincolor.com).

Heather Liljengren is the supervising seed collector and field taxonomist for the Greenbelt Native Plant Center in Staten Island—a facility of the New York City Department of Parks and Recreation. She currently manages the seed collection program and seed bank at the nursery, which provides local genetic source material for restoration projects throughout New York City.

Uli Lorimer is curator of the Native Flora Garden at Brooklyn Botanic Garden, corresponding secretary for the Torrey Botanical Society, and a regular contributor to BBG handbooks. He also teaches botany, soil science, plant conservation, and biogeography in BBG's adult education program.

Judith Larner Lowry has been the proprietor of Larner Seeds, specialists in California native plants and seeds, for the past 33 years. During that time, she has designed many homeowner restoration gardens and written two books—*Gardening with a Wild Heart* (1999), and *The Landscaping Ideas of Jays* (2007), both published by the University of California Press—as well as numerous articles.

Janet Marinelli is a science journalist who writes about plant conservation and sustainable landscape design. You can find many of her articles on her website, janetmarinelli.com. A former director of Publishing at Brooklyn Botanic Garden, her latest BBG handbook is *The Climate Conscious Gardener* (2010), which won a 2011 award from the Garden Writers Association.

Sarah Reichard is a professor at the University of Washington and director of the University of Washington Botanic Gardens, in Seattle. She has researched invasive species for more than 20 years and served 6 years on the federal government's Invasive Species Advisory Committee. She is the author of *The Conscientious Gardener: Cultivating a Garden Ethic* (University of California Press, 2011).

James L. Reveal is professor emeritus at the University of Maryland, adjunct professor of plant biology at Cornell University, and an honorary curator at the New York Botanical Garden. His research interests include floristic studies, monographic studies of the knotweed family (Polygonaceae), botanical nomenclature, and the history of New World botanical explorations.

Susan K. Pell is the director of Science at Brooklyn Botanic Garden, where she researches the evolution and taxonomy of the cashew family (Anacardiaceae). She teaches a variety of botany courses at several institutions in New York City, including Brooklyn Botanic Garden and the New York Botanical Garden.

Douglas Tallamy is professor and chair of the Department of Entomology and Wildlife Ecology at the University of Delaware, where he has written more than 70 research articles. Chief among his research goals is to better understand the many ways insects interact with plants and how such interactions determine the diversity of animal communities. He is the author of *Bringing Nature Home: How Native Plants Sustain Wildlife in Our Gardens* (Timber Press, 2007).

PHOTOS

Lori J. Allard 21 (top)

Rob Cardillo 43 (middle), 74

Russ Cohen 42 (bottom)

Alan Cressler 6, 38, 56

Christian Fischer 22 (bottom)

Fritz Geller-Grimm 43

D. Gordon and E. Robertson 55

Eric Hunt 4, 66, 95 (top), 96 (top), 97

Bill Johnson Cover, 32

Mary Keim 96 (bottom)

Uli Lorimer 2, 44, 47, 50, 80, 92, 95 (bottom), 104, 108

Elizabeth Peters 18, 98

Matt Reinbold 86

Hans Stieglitz 22 (top)

Susie VanMeter 43 (top)

Index

PROVIDING EXPERT GARDENING ADVICE FOR OVER 65 YEARS

Join Brooklyn Botanic Garden as an annual Subscriber Member and have new gardening handbooks delivered directly to you, plus BBG newsletters, mailings, and privileges at many botanic gardens across the country. Visit bbg.org/subscribe for details.

BBG Guides for a Greener Planet

World renowned for pioneering gardening information, Brooklyn Botanic Garden's award-winning guides provide practical advice in a compact format for gardeners across North America. To order other fine titles, shop online at bbg.org/handbooks or call 718-623-7280. To learn more about Brooklyn Botanic Garden, visit bbg.org.